# THE SOUL AT WORK

SEMIOTEXT(E) FOREIGN AGENTS SERIES

© 2009 by Semiotext(e) and Franco Berardi

All rights reserved. No part of this book may be reproduced, stored in a retrieval system, or transmitted by any means, electronic, mechanical, photocopying, recording, or otherwise, without prior permission of the publisher.

Published by Semiotext(e)
PO Box 629, South Pasadena, CA 91031
www.semiotexte.com

Special thanks to Andrew Drabkin, John Ebert, and Jason Smith.

Cover art by Jutta Koether, *Untitled*, 2007.
Black and white photocopy, 8 1/2" X 11".
Courtesy of the artist and Reena Spaulings Fine Art, NY.

Back Cover Photography by Simonetta Candolfi
Design by Hedi El Kholti

ISBN: 978-1-58435-076-7
Distributed by The MIT Press, Cambridge, Mass. and London, England
Printed in the United States of America

10 9 8 7 6 5 4

# THE SOUL AT WORK

FROM ALIENATION TO AUTONOMY

Franco "Bifo" Berardi

Preface by Jason Smith

Translated by Francesca Cadel and Giuseppina Mecchia

\<e\>

# Contents

Preface by Jason Smith                                           9

Introduction                                                    21

1. Labor and Alienation in the philosophy of the 1960s          27

2. The Soul at Work                                             74

3. The Poisoned Soul                                           106

4. The Precarious Soul                                         184

Conclusion                                                     207

Notes                                                          223

Preface

# Soul on Strike

The soul is the *clinamen* of the body. It is how it falls, and what makes it fall in with other bodies. The soul is its gravity. This tendency for certain bodies to fall in with others is what constitutes a world. The materialist tradition represented by Epicurus and Lucretius proposed a worldless time in which bodies rain down through the plumbless void, straight down and side-by-side, until a sudden, unpredictable deviation or swerve—*clinamen*—leans bodies toward one another, so that they come together in a lasting way. The soul does not lie beneath the skin. It is the angle of this swerve and what then holds these bodies together. It spaces bodies, rather than hiding within them; it is among them, their consistency, the *affinity* they have for one another. It is what they share in common: neither a form, nor some thing, but a rhythm, a certain way of vibrating, a resonance. Frequency, tuning or tone.

To speak of a *soul* at work is to move the center of gravity in contemporary debates about cognitive capitalism. The soul is not simply the capacity for abstraction, for the subsumption of the particular. It is an aesthetic organ as well, the exposure of thought to the contractions and dilations of space, to the quickening and lapsing of time. To say the soul is put to work is to affirm that the social brain or general intellect (to use two of Marx's phrases that have some currency in these debates) is not the primary source of value in the production process. Rather the soul as a web of attachments and tastes, attractions and inclinations. The soul is not simply the seat of intellectual operations, but the affective and libidinal forces that weave together a world: attentiveness, the ability to address, care for and appeal to others. The contemporary subject of cognitive capitalism—Bifo speaks of the cognitariat, but perhaps there are other names—is not simply a producer of knowledge and a manager of symbols. Capitalism is the mobilization of a pathos and the organization of a mood; its subject, a field of desire, a point of inflexion for an impersonal affect that circulates like a rumor. The cognitariat carries a virus.

*The Soul at Work* calls itself an experiment in "psychopathology," and it describes how something in the collective soul has seized up. The world has become heavy, thick, opaque, intransigent. A little, dark light shines through, though. Something opens up with this extinction of the possible. We no longer feel compelled to act, that is, to be effective. Our passivity almost seems like a release, a refusal, a de-activation of a system of possibles that are not ours. The possible is seen for what it is: an imposition, smothering. With the eclipse of the possible, at the point zero of depressive lapse, we are at times seized by our own potentiality: a potency that, no longer invested in vectors of realization, washes back over us.

Depression occurs, Franco "Bifo" Berardi argues, when the speed and complexity of the flows of information overwhelm the capacities of the "social brain" to manage these flows, inducing a panic that concludes, shortly thereafter, with a depressive plunge. Depression is so widespread today, Bifo argues, because the contemporary organization of production of surplus-value is founded on the phenomenon—the accumulation—of speed. In well-known pages from the *Grundrisse*, Marx spoke of a tendency, a limit point in the process of the valorization of capital: the impossible possibility that capital might circulate "without circulation *time*," at an infinite velocity, such that the passage from one moment in the circulation of capital to the next would take place at the "speed of thought." Such a capital would return to itself even before taking leave of itself, passing through all of its phases in a process encountering no obstacles, in an ideal time without time—in the blinding flash of an instant without duration, a cycle contracting into a point. No less an authority than Bill Gates restages this fantasy—a limit point of capital, toward which it strains, its vanishing point—in his *Business @ the Speed of Thought*, cited by Bifo as a contemporary formalization of this threshold, summoning the possibility of the circulation of information that would, Gates fantasizes, occur as "quickly and naturally as thought in a human being."

There is speed and there is speed. It is not simply the phenomenon of speed *as such* that plays the pathogenic role here. The social factory is just as much governed by the destabilizing experience of changes in rhythms, *differences in speeds*, whiplash-like reorientations imposed on a workforce that is flexible, precarious and permanently on-call—and equipped with the latest iPhone. This organization of work, in which just-in-time production is overseen by a permanently temporary labor force, is mirrored in the form of governance characteristic of democratic imperialism, sustained as it is by appeals to urgency, permanent mobilization, suspensions of norms: governance by crisis, rule by exception. It is impossible to separate the spheres of the economy and the political these days. In each case, a managed disorder, the administration of chaos. The social pacts and productive truces of the old welfare states are gone.

Instability is now the order of the day. Disorder, a technique of government. Depression starts to look less like a drying up of desire than a stubborn, if painful, libidinal slowdown or sabotage, a demobilization. The soul on strike.

*The Soul at Work* wants to answer this question: How did we get from the particular forms of workers' struggle in the 1960s, characterized by widespread "estrangement" of workers from the capitalist organization of production, to the situation today, in which work has become the central locus of psychic and emotional investment, even as this new libidinal economy induces an entire range of collective pathologies, from disorders of attention to new forms of dyslexia, from sudden panics to mass depression? How, in other words, have we passed from the social antagonisms of the 1960s and 1970s, when worker power was paradoxically defined by a refusal of work, its autonomy from the capitalist valorization process, and its own forms of organization—its defection from factory discipline—to the experience of the last two decades, where work has become the core of our identity, no longer economically necessary, yet vital to the constitution of the self? In short, from fleeing work to identifying with it?

Something happened in 1977. Bifo hangs his story on this mutation. It's the year when the refusal of work reaches a fever pitch in the Italian autonomia movement, the year that the logic of antagonism and worker *needs*—what Mario Tronti called the "antagonistic will" of the proletariat—gives way to a logic of *desire*, in which social productivity can no longer be accounted for in strictly economic categories, and in which the insurrectionary vectors no longer map onto the old imaginary of social war. The centrality of the category of worker needs in the struggles of the

1960s primarily took two forms. In the sphere of consumption, there was the form of direct democracy known as "political" pricing, in which neighborhoods and entire sections of cities unilaterally reduced the costs of goods and services such as housing, transportation and electricity, on the basis of a collective decision that refused any economic rationality in the determination of prices. At the point of production, the primary lever of antagonism was the wage struggle, in which worker power was exercised in a refusal to link wage levels to productivity, insisting the wage be treated as an "independent variable." The mutation represented by the events of 1977, in which the logic of needs and antagonism gives way to desire and flight, is where *The Soul at Work* really begins. For what is at stake in its story is the *aftermath* of this mass defection from factory discipline, this unilateral withdrawal from the social pact drawn up by capital and its partners, the unions and the worker parties, in view of "saving" the Italian economy after the war. It asks: how has the sphere of desire, the field of the imaginary and the affective, whose affirmation as the fundamental field of the political once led to a collective abandonment of the sphere of work, been transformed into the privileged force in the contemporary order of work, the privileged moment in the production of value? Desire braids together emotional, linguistic, cognitive and imaginary energies that affirmed themselves against the regime of work in the 1960s and 1970s, a refusal that is then paradoxically put to work by capital itself. This colonization of the soul and its desire—the entry of the soul itself into the production process—spawns paradoxical effects. It transforms labor-power into what managerial theories call human *capital*, harnessing and putting to work not an abstract, general force of labor, but the particularity, the unique combination of psychic, cognitive and affective powers

I bring to the labor process. Because this contemporary reformatting functions through the incitement of my specific creative and intellectual powers, I experience work as the segment of social life in which I am most free, most capable of realizing my desires: most *myself*.

*The Soul at Work* analyzes the contemporary dynamics of capital in its "cognitive" phase using a method it calls compositionism. This term is used by Bifo to avoid the misconceptions induced by the use of *operaismo*—workerism—to describe the specifically Italian current of Marxism he both inherits and breaks with. Though strictly speaking the phase of classical *operaismo* begins in the early 1960s and ends with the dissolution of the group *Potere Operaio* (within which Bifo militated) in 1973, the larger field of compositionist thought remains very active today, encompassing a wide range of tendencies represented by thinkers such as Paolo Virno, Antonio Negri, and Maurizio Lazzarato. This tradition is founded on three imbricated theoretical breakthroughs: the axiom asserting the primacy of worker's struggles in the development of capital, the study of the changing composition of the working class as the key for deciphering novel forms of political organization and action, and Marx's description (in the *Grundrisse*) of the emergence of the "general intellect" as a form of worker power that threatens to destroy the bases for organizing production to extort surplus-value. The first concept requires that every analysis of the changing structure of capital be understood not on the basis of the internal contradictions of capital itself, but as a certain response to, and use of, proletarian aggression: worker insubordination alone initiates restructuration on the part of capital. This response, in which the organic composition of capital—the ratio of fixed to variable capital—undergoes a mutation, induces a recomposition of the internal consistency of the working class. This axiom of the priority of worker refusal required, in turn, the development of a phenomenology of proletarian experience. This phenomenology described the changing internal composition of the various layers of the working class, identifying emerging strata that would assume a dominant role in the immediate process of production: for example, the increasing importance of the mass worker in the Fordist factory, after the hegemony of the skilled worker of earlier social compositions. On the basis of this analysis of the different strata of the working class, novel political forms of organization and action—beyond the Leninist party and its revolutionary strategy—adequate to this composition. Finally, the thesis on the "general intellect," in which Marx sees the use of automation in the production process reaching a moment when labor-time can no longer be posited as the measure of value, implies both of the preceding concepts: the move to an increasingly automated system of production is seen as a response to worker struggles around the working day, while the positing of the intellect and knowledge as a productive force implies a change within the composition of the working class, with certain sectors (in Bifo's analysis, the cognitariat) emerging as the paradigmatic form of labor. Insofar as the method of class composition is undertaken in view of seeking out novel openings in the social war—its elevation to another level of complexity and intensity—the specter of a labor process increasingly founded on the production and management of knowledge initiated, an erosion of the classical division of labor and its corresponding organizational diagrams. Placing pressure on Marx's analysis of the general intellect allowed the militants of the compositionist tradition to diagram a series of mutations in the dynamics of contemporary class antagonism. The collapse of the distinction between conception and execution, between managing production and production itself, threatened to generalize the site of conflict to society as a whole, diminishing the absolute privilege accorded the factory as the unique point of production and exploitation.

*The Soul at Work* begins from these analytical premises. Using the thesis of the general intellect as a starting point to describe the dynamics of cognitive capital, it reformats this concept to include the range of emotional, affective and aesthetic textures and experiences that are deployed in the contemporary experience of work, and gives it another name: soul. From there, *The Soul at Work* explains the emergence of the current regime of accumulation as a reaction to the intensification of proletarian refusal to work that began in the 1960s and reached its peak—the point of mass defection from the factories and the wage-relation—in 1977, with the proliferation of areas of autonomy and the supplanting of worker needs with communist desire. And most importantly, it attempts to decipher the possible forms of politics opened by a new class composition whose paradigm is the cognitive worker. What mutations in the forms and vectors of politics are implied by the definitive implosion of the Leninist schema of the Party and the revolutionary destruction of the bourgeois state? In other words, what are the possibilities of communism today, in a post-political moment when the classical forms of organization and action corresponding to an earlier class composition have withered away?

We're starting to talk about communism again these days. We don't know yet what it is, but it's what we *want*. The enigmatic final lines of *The Soul at Work* ask us to contemplate the possibility of a communism that is no longer the "principle of a new totalization," but an endless process of constituting poles of autonomy communicating via "therapeutic contagion." Politics, Bifo suggests, still belongs to the order of totality. Whether understood as the management of social conflict through the mediation of the State and the forms of juridical equivalence, or as the practice of an irreducible antagonism, the political has always been wedded to the logical and metaphysical categories of totality and negation. Communism means the withering away of the political. But the post-political era opens not onto an administration of things, as Engels once dreamed, but to what is here daringly called *therapy*—that is, with the articulation of "happy singularizations" that defect from the metropolitan factory of unhappiness.

The call-to-arms sounded by the Bolognese autonomo-punk journal *A/traverso* (founded by Bifo in 1975) was "the practice of happiness is subversive when it's collective." This call still resonates, however muffled. Today, we can add: happiness is collective only when it produces singularities. Bifo calls the contemporary organization of production in which the soul and its affective, linguistic and cognitive powers are put to work the factory of unhappiness because the primary function of the work the post-Fordist factory commands is not the creation of value but the fabrication of subjectivities—the modeling of psychic space and the induction of psychopathologies as a technique of control. In a phase of capitalist development in which the quantity of socially necessary labor is so insignificant that it can no longer seriously be considered the measure of value, the ghostly afterlife of the order of work is an entirely political necessity. Work is a matter of discipline, the production of docility. When work becomes the site of libidinal and narcissistic investment, spinning a web of abjections and dependencies that exploits rather than represses desire—we become attached and bound to our own unhappiness.

"Happiness" is a fragile word. In a book he wrote about Félix Guattari, Bifo concedes that it can sound "corny and banal," to which we might add rotten, having languished in the fetid mouths of the planetary petit bourgeoisie long enough to be tainted for all time. Our metaphysicians held it in contempt. Hegel identified it with dumb immediacy, blank as an empty page. Kant was equally clear, founding his moral philosophy on the premise that it is better to be worthy of happiness than to be happy—ethics opens in the fault between the order of value and an order of affections structured by aesthetic textures and the contingencies of space and time. Psychoanalysis taught us that happiness comes at a price: a renunciation of drives, which, far from banishing them, makes them that much nastier, turned back against us in the guise of guilt and cruel self-laceration. In the *Grundrisse*, Marx admonished Adam Smith for confusing freedom with happiness and work with necessity, sacrifice and suffering. This is true, he thundered, only from the perspective of the current regime of work, wage-labor as "externally forced labor." But if work is for us sacrifice, it can one day be "self-realization": the construction and mastery of one's own conditions of existence, freedom as self-objectification, the making of a world *as* the production of the self itself. In a society in which work is no longer organized by a small clique which has monopolized the means of production through violence, crime and economic reason, work will become seductive. Labor will be attractive, says Marx following Fourier, because it is no longer work at all but its negation and overcoming, the accumulation of joy and the collective composition of a commons. Such pleasure will not be mere play or, God forbid, "fun," but what Marx calls "damned seriousness":

"Really free working, e.g. *composing*, is at the same time precisely the most damned seriousness, the most intense exertion" (*Grundrisse*, p. 611; my italics).

The task of the communism to come is the constitution of poles of autonomy where what Marx calls the "individual's self-realization" and Bifo calls "happy singularizations" becom shared possibilities. The contemporary regime of work has produced a perfect inversion of the scenario Marx projects—work has become the site of libidinal investment, but produces pathologies and depression rather than the damned serious practice of happiness. The creation of zones of therapeutic contagion requires not only a defection from the archaic form of the wage—in which we still pretend to measure value with the time of work—but undertaking a labor on ourselves, a working through of our attachment to work. The great epoch of the refusal of work required that we go on the offensive against ourselves, that the proletariat destroy itself as a class, as labor-power. Today, we are told, this politics of destruction is replaced by a therapy that is primarily aesthetic in nature: the composition of a *refrain* that constitutes a territory subtracted from the social factory and its temporalities and rhythms. For Marx, the privileged example of really free working—happiness itself—is "composition," the construction of the communist score. Now we know: the aesthetic paradigm of the communism to come will consist in the singularization and *elaboration* of forms-of-life, a communism whose song will free the space in which it resonates, and spreads.

— Jason Smith

# Introduction

> *"Those who maintain that the soul is incorporeal are talking nonsense, because it would not be able to act upon or be acted upon if it were of such a nature; but in actuality both these functions are clearly distinguishable in the case of the soul."*
> — Epicurus, *Letter to Herodotus*, par. 67[1]

The soul I intend to discuss does not have much to do with the spirit. It is rather the vital breath that converts biological matter into an animated body.

I want to discuss the soul in a materialistic way. What the body can do, that is its soul, as Spinoza said.

In order to describe the processes of subjection arising with the formation of industrial societies, Foucault tells the story of modernity as a disciplining of the body, building the institutions and devices capable of subduing the body through the machines of social production. Industrial exploitation deals with bodies, muscles and arms. Those bodies would not have any value if they weren't animated, mobile, intelligent, reactive.

The rise of post-Fordist modes of production, which I will call Semiocapitalism, takes the mind, language and creativity as its primary tools for the production of value. In the sphere of digital production, exploitation is exerted essentially on the semiotic flux produced by human time at work.

It is in this sense that we speak of immaterial production. Language and money are not at all metaphors, and yet they are immaterial. They are nothing, and yet can do everything: they move, displace, multiply, destroy. They are the soul of Semiocapital.

If today we want to continue the genealogical work of Michel Foucault, we have to shift the focus of theoretical attention towards the automatisms of mental reactivity, language and imagination, and therefore towards the new forms of alienation and precariousness of the mental work occurring in the Net.

In this book I will examine anew the Marxist language which was dominant in the 1960s, trying to reestablish its vitality with respect to the languages of post-structuralism, schizoanalysis and cyberculture.

Despite the fact that the term "soul" is never used in the language of that historical period, I want to use it—metaphorically and even a bit ironically—in order to rethink the core of many questions referring to the issue of alienation. In the Hegelian vision this issue is defined by the relationship between human essence and activity, while in the materialist vision of Italian Workerism (*Operaismo*), alienation is defined as the relationship between human time and capitalist value, that is to say as the reification of both body and soul. In the Hegelian-Marxist tradition of the 20th Century, the concept of "alienation" refers specifically to the relation existing between corporeality and human essence. For Hegel the word "alienation" (*Entäusserung*) refers to the self becoming other, to the historical and mundane separation existing between the Being and the existent.

In Marx, the concept of alienation signifies the split between life and labor, the split between the workers' physical activity and their humanity, their essence as humans. Young Marx, the author of the *1844 Manuscripts* who was the main reference for the radical philosophy of the 1960s, attributes a pivotal role to the notion of alienation.

In Marx's parlance, as in Hegel before, alienation (*Entäusserung*) and estrangement (*Entfremdung*) are two terms that define the same process from two different standpoints. The first one defines the sense of loss felt by consciousness when faced with an object in the context of capital's domination; the second term refers to the confrontation between the consciousness and the scene of exteriority, and to the creation of an autonomous consciousness based on the refusal of its own dependence on work.

Italian Workerist thought overturned the vision of Marxism that was dominant in those years: the working class is no longer conceived as a passive object of alienation, but instead as the active subject of a refusal capable of building a community starting out from its estrangement from the interests of capitalistic society.

Alienation is then considered not as the loss of human authenticity, but as estrangement from capitalistic interest, and therefore as a necessary condition for the construction—in a space estranged from and hostile to labor relations—of an ultimately human relationship.

In the context of French Post-Structuralism, a similar overturning of the traditional vision of clinical alienation was finding its way: schizophrenia, considered by psychiatry only as the separation and loss of self-consciousness, is rethought by Félix Guattari in totally new terms. Schizophrenia is not the passive effect of a scission of consciousness, but rather a form of consciousness that is multiple, proliferating and nomadic.

In this book I want to compare the conceptual framework of the '60s based on the Hegelian concepts of Alienation and Totalization to the conceptual framework of our present, which is based on the concepts of biopolitics and of psychopathologies of desire.

In the first part of the book I want to describe the relationship between philosophy and theories of labor in the '60s. In the wave of a Hegelian Renaissance and the constitution of Critical Theory, industrial labor was seen from the point of view of alienation, and the rebellion of industrial workers against exploitation was seen as the beginning of a process of disalienation.

In the second part of the book I will account for the progressive mentalization of working processes, and the consequent enslavement of the soul. Putting the soul to work: this is the new form of alienation. Our desiring energy is trapped in the trick of self-enterprise, our libidinal investments are regulated according to economic rules, our attention is captured in the precariousness of virtual networks: every fragment of mental activity must be transformed into capital. I will describe the channeling of Desire in the process of valorization and the psychopathological implications of the subjugation of the soul to work processes.

In the third part I will retrace the evolution of several radical theories, from the idealistic concept of Alienation to the analytical concept of psychopathology. I will also compare the philosophy of Desire (Deleuze and Guattari) with the philosophy of Simulation (Baudrillard), in order to underscore their differences but also their complementarity.

In the fourth part of the book I will try to outline the effects of the precarization of labor—especially of cognitive labor—and the effects of the biopolitical subjugation of language and affections.

In the conclusion, I will comment on the current collapse of the integrated psycho-machinic organism that is the Global Economy. The collapse of the Global Economy following the recent financial crack could be the opening of a new era of autonomy and emancipation for the soul.

# 1

# Labor and Alienation in the philosophy of the 1960s

**Workers and students united in their fight**

In the 1960s Marxism was a pole of attraction for different schools of thought, such as structuralism, phenomenology and neo-Hegelianism—and the great international explosion of 1968 can be read as the point of arrival for a theoretical work that had been developing on many conceptual levels, as the crossing of different projects.

In the year 1968, with a synchronicity previously unheard of in human history, we can see great masses of people all over the world—workers and students—fighting against both the capitalist *moloch* and the authoritarianism of the socialist world.

From this perspective, the 1968 movements were the first phenomenon of conscious globalization. First of all, internationalism was present in the consciousness of its agents. At Berkeley you would mobilize for Vietnam, while in Shanghai there were rallies of solidarity with the Parisian students. In Prague students were fighting against Soviet authoritarianism, while in Milan the enemy was the capitalist state—but the positive meaning emerging from the different movements was the same everywhere.

The meaning of those movements was the emergence of a new historical alliance. It was an alliance between mass intellectual labor and the workers' refusal of industrial labor.

Despite being deeply rooted in the history of the twentieth century, despite being ideologically animated by different schools of thought embedded in the twentieth century, 1968 marks the beginning of the exit from industrial societies, the beginning of a process leading to the disembodiment of the modern Nation-State.

Workers and students: this binomial marks a new quality in the composition of general social labor and implies the articulation of a new kind of innovative potentiality with respect to 20th-century history.

The emergence of intellectual, technical and scientific labor is a sign of the decade: the political power of the 1968 movements derives from the students having become mass: they had become a part of the general social labor force characterized by a strong homogeneity at a world level.

In those same 1960s, the industrial working class showed a growing estrangement towards the organization of labor, until this estrangement became open insubordination and organized revolt.

In some productive sectors, as for instance in the car production cycle, labor had a mass depersonalized character: it is in these sectors that the refusal of work exploded more significantly. In the mid 1970s the entire European car production cycle was stormed by waves of workers' fights, sabotage and absenteeism, until a technological reorganization aimed at the reassertion of capitalist rule defeated the worker's power. The technical restructuration implied the substitution of human labor with machines, the automation of entire productive cycles and the subjugation of mental activity.

"Workers and students united in their fight" is perhaps the most significant slogan of the so-called "Italian Red Biennium." In 1968 and 1969 these words were shouted in thousands of rallies, meetings, strikes and demonstrations: they were much more than a political and ideological alliance or a superficial form of solidarity. They were the sign of the organic integration of labor and intelligence, they meant the conscious *constitution* of the general intellect that Marx had discussed in his *Grundrisse*.

The theoretical problems, the sociological imagination and the philosophical critique articulated during those years are directly implied in the social and cultural developments of the students' movement—of its cultural and productive convergence with the movement based on the refusal of industrial labor.

Italian neo-Marxism, often denominated "Workerism," is a school of thought focused on the relation between working class struggles and intellectual and technological transformations.

**The modern intellectual**

Today the word "intellectual" has lost much of the meaning it had throughout the twentieth century, when around this word coalesced not only issues of social knowledge, but also ethics and politics. In the second half of the twentieth century intellectual labor completely changed its nature, having been progressively absorbed into the domain of economic production. Once digital technologies made the connection of individual fragments of cognitive labor possible, the parceled intellectual labor was subjected to the value production cycle. The ideological and political forms of the left wing, legacy of the 20th Century, have become inefficient in this new context.

In the context of the past bourgeois society, in the sphere of modern Enlightenment, the intellectual was not defined by his/her social condition, but as representative of a system of universal values. The role attributed to intellectuals by the Enlightenment was to establish and guarantee—by the exercise of rationality—the respect for human rights, equality and the universality of law.

The modern figure of the intellectual finds philosophical justification in Kant's thought. Within that context, the intellectual emerges as a figure independent from social experience, or at least not socially influenced in the ethical and cognitive choices s/he makes. As the bearer of a universal human rationality, the enlightened intellectual can be considered as the social determination of Kant's "I think." The intellectual is the guarantor of a thought freed from any boundaries, the expression of a universally human rationality. In this sense s/he is the guarantor of democracy. Democracy cannot stem from any cultural root or belonging, but only from a boundless horizon of possibilities and choices, from opportunities of access and citizenship for every person as semiotic agent and subject, who exchanges signs in order to have access to universal rationality. In this sense the figure of the intellectual is in opposition to the Romantic notion of the people, or rather escapes from such a notion. Universal Thought, from which the modern adventure of democracy was born, is indeed an escape from historicity and the territoriality of culture. Democracy cannot have the mark of a culture, of a people, of a tradition: it has to be a groundless play, invention and convention, rather than an assertion of belonging.

Both historical and dialectical materialism assert a completely different vision: the intellectual becomes the agent of a specific historic message, destined to descend from the history of thought to the history of social classes. In the eleventh of his *Theses on*

*Feuerbach*, referring to the role that knowledge must have in the historical process, Marx wrote:

> "The philosophers have *only interpreted* the world in various ways; the point, however, is to *change* it."[1]

Marxist intellectuals conceive themselves as instruments of a historical process aimed at producing a society without classes. The Communist project makes theory a material power and knowledge an instrument to change the world. Only insofar as s/he takes part in the fight towards the abolition of classes and wage-earning labor does the intellectual in fact become the agent of a universal mission.

The role of intellectuals is crucial in 20th-Century political philosophy, specifically in Communist revolutionary thought, beginning with Lenin. In his book *What is to Be Done?* Lenin attributes the task of leading the historic process to the intellectuals, in the interest of the working class. The intellectual, being a free spirit, is not the agent of a social interest but serves the emerging interest, s/he identifies with the party which is the ultimate collective intellectual. For Lenin, intellectuals are not a social class, they have no specific interest to support. They can become agents and organizers of a revolutionary consciousness stemming from philosophical thought. In this sense, intellectuals are closest to the pure becoming of the Spirit, to the Hegelian development of self-consciousness. On the other hand, the workers, despite being the agents of a social interest, can only move from a purely economic phase (Hegel's self-consciousness of the social being) to the conscious political phase (self-consciousness *per se*) through the political structure of the party, which embodies and transmits the philosophical heritage.

With Gramsci, the meditation on intellectuals becomes more specific and concrete, despite the fact that Gramsci still thinks of a figure linked to the humanistic intellectual, estranged from any dynamic of production. Only in the second half of the 20th century does the figure of the intellectual start changing its nature, because its function becomes heavily incorporated in the technological process of production.

In Sartre's work, which is extremely important for the formation of the cultural atmosphere leading to 1968, the notion of the intellectual is still bound to the perspective of consciousness, rather than to a productive and social perspective:

> "*The intellectual is someone who meddles in what is not his business* and claims to question both received truths and the accepted behaviour inspired by them, in the name of a global conception of man and of society [...]. I would suggest that the scientists working on atomic scission in order to perfect the techniques of atomic warfare should not be called 'intellectuals': they are scientists and nothing more. But if these same scientists, terrified by the destructive power of the devices they have helped to create, join forces and sign a manifesto alerting public opinion to the dangers of the atomic bomb, they become intellectuals [...]. They stray outside their field of competence—constructing bombs is one thing, but evaluating their use is another [...]. They do not protest against the use of the bomb on the grounds of any technical defects it may have, but in the name of a highly controversial system of values that sees human life as its supreme standard."[2]

For Sartre the intellectual is s/he who chooses to engage in favor of universal causes, without being socially destined to this engagement. But once intellectual labor becomes a directly productive function, once scientists become workers applied to the machine of cognitive production, and poets workers applied to advertising, the machine of imaginative production, there is no universal function to be fulfilled anymore. Intellectual labor becomes a part of the autonomous process of the capital.

In 1968 the shift in the problem was implicit, even if only a tiny part of the movement was aware of it.

As a consequence of mass access to education and, the technical and scientific transformation of production, the role of intellectuals has been redefined: they are no longer a class independent from production, nor free individuals assuming the task of a purely ethical and freely cognitive choice, but a mass social subject, tending to become an integral part of the general process of production. Paolo Virno writes of "mass intellectuality," in order to understand the social subjectivity corresponding to the massification of intellectual competences in an advanced industrial society. In the 1960s, the rise of the student movements was the sign of this change within the social scene on which the new figure of the intellectual was emerging.

## The Italian "Workerist" perspective

As we have said, the change of perspective maturing by the end of the 1960s is analyzed in an original way by the so-called Italian Workerism (Mario Tronti, Raniero Panzieri, Toni Negri, Romano Alquati, Sergio Bologna). I would prefer to define this school of thought as "compositionism," since its essential theoretical contribution consists in the reformulation of the issue of political organization in terms of social composition.

*Compositionism* redefines the Leninist notion of the party as collective intellectual, leaving behind the very notion of the intellectual while proposing a new reading of the Marxist notion of "general intellect." Marx had written of *general intellect* in a passage of his *Grundrisse* known as the "*Fragment on the machines*":

> "Nature builds no machines, no locomotives, railways, electric telegraphs, self-acting mules etc. These are products of human industry; natural material transformed into organs of the human will over nature, or of human participation in nature [...]. They are *organs of the human brain, created by the human hand*; the power of knowledge, objectified. The development of fixed capital indicates to what degree general social knowledge has become a *direct force of production*, and to what degree, hence, the conditions of the process of social life itself have come under the control of the general intellect and been transformed in accordance with it. To what degree the powers of social production have been produced, not only in the form of knowledge, but also as immediate organs of social practice, of the real life process."[3]

At the time of the communist revolutions, in the first part of the twentieth century, the Marxist-Leninist tradition ignored the concept of *general intellect*, therefore conceiving the intellectual function as exteriority and as a political direction determined within the purely spiritual domain of philosophy. But during the post-industrial transformation of production the general intellect emerged as a central productive force. At the end of the 20th century, thanks to digital technologies and the constitution of a global telematic network, the general social process is redefined as "*general intellect*," and the Leninist idea of the party is forever put aside. Gramsci's notion of the organic intellectual is also losing its concrete reference, since it is based on the intellectuals' attachment to an ideology, while nowadays what is important is the creation of a new social sphere, that we might want to call "cognitariat," representing the social subjectivity of the "*general intellect*."

If we want to define the crux of today's mutations, we must focus on the social function of cognitive labor. Intellectual labor is no longer a social function separated from general labor, but it becomes a transversal function within the entire social process, it becomes the creation of technical and linguistic interfaces ensuring the fluidity both of the productive process and of social communication.

**Subjectivity and alienation**

In the 1960s, we could find three tendencies within the field of Marxist thought:

The first emphasized the young Marx's thought, his humanistic vocation, and the issue of subjectivity: it underlined its continuity with Hegel, specifically with his *The Phenomenology of Spirit*.

The second focused mainly on *Capital*, and on Marx's work after his epistemological rupture with Hegelianism: this tendency can be linked to structuralism.

The third tendency discovered and emphasized the importance of *Grundrisse*, therefore the concept of composition and general intellect, while maintaining conceptual links with phenomenology.

Karl Marx's early works were published and distributed by the institutions assigned to their scholastic and dogmatic conservation (mainly by the *Institute for Marxism-Leninism*) very late. Marx's *Manuscripts of 1844* were published only in 1957, in Karl Marx and Friedrich Engels' *Werke*, published by Dietz Verlag in Berlin. This work was considered a scandal, as the revelation of another Marx, different from the severe author of *Capital*. Economic materialism was diluted by a consideration of the workers' subjectivity that was absent from the geometric structure of Marx's major works.

The atmosphere created in 1956 by the twentieth Congress of CPUS opened the way to a revaluation of the currents of critical Marxism, radical Hegelianism, and so-called humanistic Marxism.

Beginning in the 1950s, Sartre had led a critical battle against dogmatism and determinism within Marxist studies, opening the way to a humanistic formulation and a revaluation of subjectivity against dialectic reductionism. But Sartre's philosophical point of departure was a radically anti-Hegelian existentialism.

Even within the Hegelian dialectical field there had been instances in favor of a revaluation of subjectivity. The new interest in Hegel's thought, first in the 1920s, then through the studies of the Frankfurt School and finally with the *Hegel Renaissance* of the 1960s, led to the emergence of the issue of subjectivity and of the specifically human within the historical process.

In order to understand the progressive emergence of the theme of subjectivity, we can start rereading Marx's early work, so relevant during the 1960s in Marxist studies and, more generally, in the field of critical culture.

At the center of young Marx's thought—and significantly at the center also of the political and philosophical problems of the 1960s—is the notion of alienation. Let's try to understand the meaning of this word:

"The worker becomes poorer the more wealth he produces, the more his production increases in power and extent. The worker becomes an ever cheaper commodity the more commodities he produces. The *devaluation* of the human world grows in direct proportion to the *increase in value* of the world of things. [...] The worker is related to the *product of labour* as to an *alien* object. For it is clear that, according to this premise, the more the worker exerts himself in his work, the more powerful the alien, objective world becomes which he brings into being over against himself, the poorer he and his inner world become, and the less they belong to him."[4]

Marx's attention is focused on the anthropological consequences of working conditions within the structure of capitalistic production. What happens to the human being trapped in a wage-earning productive relation? This is what essentially happens: the more the wage earner's energy is invested in productive activity, the more s/he reinforces the power of the enemy, of capital, and the less is left for oneself. In order to survive, in order to receive a wage, workers have to renounce their humanity, the human investment of their time and energies.

The concept of alienation derives from Marx's ongoing meditation on the religion question and on the thought of Ludwig Feuerbach:

"It is the same in religion. The more man puts into God, the less he retains within himself. The worker places his life in the object; but now it no longer belongs to him, but to the object [...]. What the product of his labour is, he is not. Therefore, the greater this product, the less is he himself. The externalisation of the worker in his product means not only that his labour becomes an object, an *external* existence, but that it exists *outside him*, independently of him and alien to him, and begins to confront him as an autonomous power; that the life which he has bestowed on the object confronts him as hostile and alien."[5]

In the social situation of the 1960s, with the full development of industrial societies, mature capitalism produced goods in growing quantities, created conditions of wealth for consumers, and kept the promise of a more satisfactory economic life for all. But the satisfaction of economic needs was accompanied by a progressive loss of life, of pleasure, of time for oneself. Millions of people were experiencing this in their life: the more powerful the economic machine, the more the life of the worker becomes miserable. This awareness spread largely in those years and Marx's early works were able to interpret it. The concept of alienation defines this thematic field and it came to Marx from the Hegelian conceptual context, authorizing a Hegelian reading of the entire discourse.

The thematic scenery we can perceive behind the *Manuscripts of 1844* is that of Hegelian idealism. And indeed, the discovery of this work in the 1960s was accompanied by the large diffusion of the critical thought of the Frankfurt School and of a humanism of idealist derivation.

The conceptual scheme of alienation is idealist in so far as it presupposes human authenticity, an essence that has been lost, negated, taken away, suspended. Therefore communism is thought by the young Marx as the restoration of an authentically human essence that was negated by the relation of capitalist production. In other terms: the communist revolutionary process is conceived as the restoration of an original identity whose perversion, temporary obliteration—whose "alienation," in other words—is represented by the workers' present condition.

> "Communism therefore as the complete return of man to himself as a *social* (i.e., human) being—a return accomplished consciously and embracing the entire wealth of previous development. This communism, as fully developed naturalism, equals humanism, and as fully developed humanism equals naturalism; it is the genuine resolution of the conflict between man and nature and between man and man—the true resolution of the strife between existence and essence, between objectification and self-confirmation, between freedom and necessity, between the individual and the species. Communism is the riddle of history solved, and it knows itself to be this solution."[6]

The ideological vice of the young Marx's formulation resides entirely in this presupposition of a generic human essence whose negation would be represented by the concrete history of the conditions of the working classes. But where does this presupposition find its basis, if not in the idealistic hypostasis of human essence? Here Marx's language reveals its conceptual continuity with Hegel's, and its persistence within the idealistic problematic.

In order to better understand the idealistic function of the concept of alienation, and the connected idealistic machinery revolving around the notion of a generic human essence—and of historic subjectivity—we need to refer to Hegel's work, to the very dynamic of the Hegelian language:

"Over against the I as abstract being-for-itself, there stands likewise its *inorganic nature,* as being [*seyend*]. The I relates itself negatively to it [its inorganic nature], and annuls it as the unity of both—but in such a way that the I first shapes that abstract being-for-itself as its Self, sees its own form [in it] and thus consumes itself as well. In the element of being as such, the existence and range of natural needs is a multitude of needs. The things serving to satisfy those needs are worked up [*verarbeitet*], their universal inner possibility posited [expressed] as outer possibility, as form. This processing [*Verarbeiten*] of things is itself manysided, however; it is consciousness making itself into a thing. But in the element of universality, it is such that it becomes an abstract labor. The needs are many. The incorporation of their multiplicity in the I, i.e., labor, is an abstraction of universal models (*Bilder*), yet [it is] a self-propelling process of formation (*Bilden*)."[7]

The alienated character of labor is linked here explicitly (even if in a very obscure, typically Hegelian language) to the becoming of the Mind, and to the dialectic of being-for-itself and of being-for-the-other. This way of thinking absorbs the entire (concrete, historical) dialectic of labor and of capitalistic expropriation within the idealistic dialectic of subject and substance. In Hegel's *Phenomenology of Spirit* we read:

"Further, the living Substance is being which is in truth Subject, or, what is the same, is in truth actual only in so far as it is the movement of positing itself, or is the mediation of its self-othering with itself. This Substance is, as Subject, pure simple negativity [...]. Only this self-restoring sameness, or this reflection in otherness within itself—not an original or immediate unity as such—is the True. It is the process of its own becoming, the circle that presupposes its end as its goal, having its end also as its beginning; and only by being worked out to its end, is it actual."[8]

Despite his critique of idealist philosophy, in his *Manuscripts of 1844* Marx is still trapped in the Hegelian conceptual system, when he proposes to think of communism as "resolution of the strife between existence and essence," attributing a transcendent and eschatological character to communism, as if there were a radical beyond representing the truth to be realized outside the contradictions of the existing. This theological vision of communism is not without consequences in the history of the workers' movements.

**Alienation between history and ontology**

The great success known by critical theory, whose foundations can be found in the pages of authors like Horkheimer, Adorno and Marcuse, can be understood in the context of this idealistic renaissance.

The issue of alienation is at the core of the critical thought of the Frankfurt School, and also—although with a completely different inflection—of the Existentialists' reflection, especially in Jean-Paul Sartre, although from different points of view. Referring to the two most significant examples within existentialism and critical thought, Sartre's and Marcuse's standpoints—though radically different—exist on the same terrain: the humanistic foundations for the process of liberation from capitalism. Examining these divergent positions will allow us to get to the heart of the matter that is important for us: the vitality of the philosophical notion of alienation and its exhaustion during the historical and political battles of the 1960s. Alienation is considered by the existentialist formulations as an unavoidable and constitutive element of the human condition, since otherness (condition of the social relation) and reification (condition of the productive relation) both imply a loss of self. In the social relation, in the presence of otherness, is implicit a certain form of alienation, of uneasiness. *L'enfer c'est les autres* (Hell is other people), declares Existentialism. The others are the hell of alienation, independently from the social condition we are living in.

Hegel, Marx, and the Frankfurt School, on the other hand, share the belief that alienation is not ontologically identified with otherness and reification, but constitutes instead a historically determined form, and therefore it is possible to overcome it historically.

On this matter, in his book on the Frankfurt School entitled *The Dialectical Imagination*, Martin Jay wrote:

> "To Marcuse, Sartre had erroneously made absurdity into an ontological rather than a historical condition. As a result, he fell back into an idealistic internalization of freedom as something opposed to the outside, heteronomous world. Despite his avowed revolutionary intentions, his politics and his philosophy were totally at odds. By locating freedom in the *pour-soi* could become *en-soi* (being-in-itself, or *an-sich*), Sartre severed subjectivity from objectivity in a way that denied reconciliation even as a utopian possibility. Moreover, by overemphasizing the freedom of the subject and ignoring the constraints produced by historical condition, Sartre had

become an unwitting apologist for the status quo. Arguing as Sartre did that men chose their fate, even if it was a horrible one, was monstrous [...]. To Marcuse, the entire project of an 'existentialist' philosophy without an a priori idea of essence was impossible."[9]

In *Reason and Revolution*, one of Herbert Marcuse's most important texts, we read:

"The worker alienated from his product is at the same time alienated from himself. His labor itself becomes no longer his own, and the fact that it becomes the property of another bespeaks an expropriation that touches the very essence of man. Labor in its true form is a medium for man's true self-fulfillment, for the full development of his potentialities."[10]

Here Marcuse links two very different topics as if they were the same one: the development of potentialities (concretely determined in the social and technical history of the conflict between workers and capital) and human self-realization.

The first is a material and precise issue, while the second is instead a quintessentially idealistic, essentialist issue.

On the contrary, according to what Sartre maintains in his *Critique of Dialectical Reason*, alienation is nothing other than the intrinsic modality of alterity, which is the constitutive form of the social relation and human condition.

While Marcuse considers alienation as a historical form that could be overcome historically, Sartre wants to ground anthropologically the historic condition itself: he locates history's anthropological roots in scarcity and alterity.

Sartre situates himself outside the Hegelian field, since he does not consider alienation to be an historical separation between existence and essence. This is why he does not conceive the idea of an overcoming, of an exit from the anthropological dimensions of scarcity and alterity. He refuses the theological vision of communism that dialectical materialism had built. Scarcity, Sartre maintains, is anthropologically constitutive of the historic relation.

**Estrangement *versus* alienation**

The philosophical style of Italian Workerism—or, as I prefer to call it, *Compositionism*—beginning with Panzieri and Tronti's works, presents the issue of alienation in radically different terms than those of humanism, freeing itself from both the neo-Hegelian and Frankfurt School's vision and its existentialist Sartrian version.

According to the humanistic vision, that had developed in opposition to so-called *diamat*, the dialectical materialist dogmatism of orthodox Marxism-Leninism, alienation is the separation between human beings, the loss of human essence in historical existence.

Compositionism, even if in complete agreement with the critique of the Stalinist *diamat*, dialectical and historicist dogmatism, does not anticipate any restoration of humanity, does not proclaim any human universality, and bases its understanding of humanity on class conflict.

Compositionism overturns the issue implicit in the question of alienation. It is precisely thanks to the radical inhumanity of the workers' existence that a human collectivity can be founded, a community no longer dependent on capital. It is indeed the estrangement of the workers from their labor, the feeling of alienation and its refusal, that are the bases for a human collectivity autonomous from capital.

In the writings published in the magazines *Classe operaia* (*Working Class*), and then in *Potere operaio* (*Worker Power*), the word "estrangement" replaces the word "alienation," which inevitably alludes to a previous human essence, lost in the historical process, waiting for a synthesis capable of reestablishing it, of calling it into being as a positivity. Labor is no longer considered to be the natural condition of human sociality, but a specific historical condition that needs to undergo a political critique. A critique of "laborism" was already present in Marx's early writings:

> "It [*labour*] is, therefore, not the satisfaction of a need but a mere *means* to satisfy needs outside itself. Its alien character is clearly demonstrated by the fact that as soon as no physical or other compulsion exists, it is shunned like the plague. External labour, labour in which man alienates himself, is a labour of self-sacrifice, of mortification. Finally, the external character of labour for the worker is demonstrated by the fact that it belongs not to him but to another, and that in it he belongs not to himself but to another. Just as in religion the spontaneous activity of the human imagination, the human brain, and the human heart, detaches itself from the individual and reappears as the alien activity of a god or of a devil, so the activity of the worker is not his own spontaneous activity. It belongs to another, it is a loss of his self."[11]

Labor is an activity estranged from the existence of the workers that is imposed on everyday life by the construction of disciplinary structures created over the course of the entire history of modern civilization. Only the estrangement from labor makes liberatory dynamics possible, shifting the flow of desire from (industrial) repetition towards (cognitive) difference. *The concept of estrangement implies an intentionality that is determined by an estranged behavior.*

Estranged from what? From all forms of labor dependent on capital.

Workers do not suffer from their alienation when they can transform it into active estrangement, that is to say, into refusal.

> "The working class confronts its own labor as capital, as a hostile force, as an enemy—this is the point of departure not only for the antagonism, but for the organization of the antagonism. If the alienation of the worker has any meaning, it is a highly revolutionary one. The organization of alienation: This is the only possible direction in which the party can lead the spontaneity of the class. The goal remains that of refusal, at a higher level: It becomes active and collective, a political refusal on a mass scale, organized and planned. Hence, the immediate task of working-class organization is to overcome passivity."[12]

The alienation Tronti discusses is not described in humanistic terms (loss of the human essence) but a condition of estrangement from the mode of production and its rules, as refusal of work. The Workerist-Compositionist thinking style distinguishes itself for this overturning of humanistic connotations: what is seen by the negative thought of humanistic derivation as a sign of alienation, is seen by the Workerist-Compositionists as a sign of estrangement, a refusal to identify with the general interest of the capitalistic economy. That is to say, it is seen as the condition of those who rebel assuming their partial humanity as a point of strength, a premise of a higher social form, of a higher form of humanity, and not as the condition of those who are forced to renounce their essential humanity.

Tronti writes of the working class as a "rude pagan race," addressing Marcuse's idealism and the irrelevance of the humanistic and theological perspectives that it projects onto the reality of proletarian social composition, its working conditions, but also on the process of socialization and struggle that workers are able to effectuate in metropolitan areas.

**Tronti and Marcuse**

In one of his most influential books, *One Dimensional Man*, published in the U.S. in 1964, Herbert Marcuse foresees for the working class a destiny of integration into the capitalistic system. Consequently, he sees the necessity, for those willing to change the social order, of shifting their political attention towards the domain of extra-productive marginalities and away from the direct domain of the productive relation. Marcuse's analysis had consistent effects on the youth culture of the time, since it seemed to anticipate the student movements as a leading force of the anti-capitalistic struggle in order to replace an already integrated working class that is already irretrievable for the purpose of revolutionary conflict.

> "In Marcuse's book, the youth of 1968 found the topics and the words needed to give definite form to an idea that had already been circulating in Europe for a while, but in a less articulate way. It was the idea that European societies, only twenty years after Fascism and war had ended, were already blocked societies. [...] They were blocked even at the level of hope for future changes, since youth considered the major

part of the working class, with its representative parties belonging to the traditional left, as being already integrated in the existing social system, and therefore no longer credible, a historical subject incapable of imposing radical innovations."[13]

It was from the students, who were not involved in the productive process—or at least who thought so—that came the hope for change that the working class had lost, since unionization, economicism, improved material conditions and consumerism had produced an effect of social integration into the capitalistic system. This idea was largely circulated in those years and was part of the students' consciousness.

The working class has lost any capacity to be autonomous, caught as it is in the web of consumer society: thus Marcuse described American and European societies. In the last analysis, what Marcuse forecasted in 1964 was a period of growing social peace, where the students would have to act as the bearers of a threatened humanistic consciousness.

> "A comfortable, smooth, reasonable, democratic unfreedom prevails in advanced industrial civilization, a token of technical progress."[14]

Technical development and the functional principle produce a social integration whose effect is the cancellation of conflictual and potentially revolutionary dynamics. The society of affluence was then perceived as a harnessing of human authenticity.

> "The new technological work-world thus enforces a weakening of the negative position of the working class: the latter no

longer appears to be the living contradiction to the established society. [...] Domination is transfigured into administration."[15]

Nowadays, a few decades later, we can see important elements of prefiguration in Marcuse's discourse. The statement "domination is transfigured into administration" needs to be rethought in the new light of the creation of a system of economical and financial automatisms apparently without alternatives. Rereading Marcuse could be useful today, but in the 1960s the diffusion of his work had negative consequences, at least from the standpoint of Mario Tronti.

First of all his thought separated in a mechanical way—in the same way as the Leninist tradition—wage struggles, described as implicitly economicist and integrated, and a true political revolutionary fight.

Secondly it led to the exaltation of the separation of the student figure from the cycle of capitalistic production.

In the Workerist magazines of the 1960s, specifically in *Quaderni rossi* (*Red Notebooks*), *Classe operaia* (*Working Class*) and finally *Potere operaio* (*Workers' Power*), the wage struggle is valorized as a political fight. The workers' movement is recognized as an a-ideological movement able to destabilize the political equilibriums of capital.

The fact that the workers' struggle focuses on the wage, according to the positions expressed in *Potere operaio*, does not mean that this fight is to be considered integrated and subaltern. On the contrary: everything depends on the way in which the wage struggle is conceived, organized and directed. If wages are considered as a variable dependant on capitalistic development, a variable that must be compatible with profit, both on a fiscal and a political level, then of course they are not a lever that could overturn or transform anything. But if wages are understood as political instruments of attack and radical redistribution of social wealth, if wages are considered a factor in the conflict between workers and capital (at the level of the conflict on the exchange value of the use value of the labor force), then they end up becoming the main instrument in a conflict in which economical and political dimensions are aggressively linked to the perspective of worker autonomy from capitalistic development and hegemony.

Workerist theory refuses the notion of consumerism, since it considers the workers' consumption in a "pagan" and rude way as a form of appropriation destined to open a front line of radical and political clash.

As for the students and their movements, Workerist theory anticipates an idea that will bear fruit some time later: students are a section of social labor, they are labor in the making, a central factor in the change of capital's organic composition. Therefore the students' struggle is not celebrated as an ideological fight, and even less as a substitute for the workers' fight. It is celebrated instead as specific movement in a social sector internal to the dynamics of productive labor.

While from Marcuse's perspective students were considered as agents of an action without causes or direct consequences at the level of social production, Workerist theory sees the students from the very beginning as part of the general labor force: labor force in progress, expropriated of its knowledge just as much as workers are expropriated of the products of their work.

While humanistic theories, specifically Marcuse's, believe that it is possible to judge the spontaneity of workers' behaviors in the name of a principle of human universality, or historical teleology, Tronti answers that there is no universal principle from which workers' behaviors derive, or according to which the workers' movement could be judged. The workers' position is rather one of estrangement, situating itself outside the logic and general interest of capitalistic society.

In the discourse developed in the journal *Classe operaia*, wages are considered a political weapon, in the sense that immediate class behavior is not compatible with capitalist order.

The Workerist vision is founded on the idea that in the social process what comes first is the workers' resistance to capital and the refusal to work. Everything else (political apparatuses, technological models) depends on the relations of force between classes.

## Structuralism and *Das Kapital*

Marx's early work is at the center of both Marcuse's and Sartre's anthropological meditation, even if they develop in directions bearing completely opposite results. Marcuse starts from an anthropology of the essence and therefore conceives the historical process as the restoration of a negated totality, while Sartre starts from the *condition of alterity and scarcity*, as the anthropological premise of historical becoming: he considers both the historical and the existential processes as destined to a failure from which only the moment of fusionality will be saved.

Louis Althusser's *For Marx* marks a new shift in Marxist studies, focusing its attention far away from the early works to stress instead the epistemological break that brings Marx's theory—in mature Marxism and specifically in *Capital*—outside the Hegelian sphere.

Structure then, not history, plays the major role, since it is not at the historical level, but at the structural one that the process of knowledge is founded.

*For Marx* is a declaration of war against Marxist Humanism, or at least against its idealistic implications. As a matter of fact this book gets rid of any pretence of considering Marx's theory as a simple "overturning" of the Hegelian system.

If we want to exit the Hegelian field of problems, we have to let go of the dialectic, we have to abandon the idea of an original truth to be restored, both on the level of the self-realization of the spirit and of the self-assertion of radical Humanism.

After *For Marx* Althusser published *Reading Capital*, a book that proposes a structuralist method aimed at understanding the capitalistic process and stressing the deep connection existing between labor and knowledge.

First of all, Althusser reproposes to keep some distance from the humanism of the young Marx:

> "The Young Marx of the *1844 Manuscripts* read the human essence at sight, immediately, in the transparency of its alienation. *Capital*, on the contrary, exactly measures a distance and an internal dislocation (*décalage*) in the real, inscribed in its *structure*, a distance and a dislocation such as to make their own effects themselves illegible […] the text of history is not a text in which a voice (the Logos) speaks, but the inaudible and illegible notation of the effects of a structure of structures."[16]

The concept of alienation shows the process by which the identical is restored. Against its grain, we can then clearly see the traces of Reason as it cleverly opens a way throughout the vicissitudes of history, as the history of the overturning of the alienated condition.

Overturning, overcoming, making true: an entire litany of Hegelian terms that constantly refer to the possibility of reading history through reason. The point is not that of overturning or overcoming (in the specific Hegelian sense of the word *auf-hebung*, which means to realize through a negation capable of abolishing and maintaining at the same time). The point is conceiving action (and also theoretical practices) as production, where producing means:

> "Making manifest what is latent, but which really means transforming (in order to give a pre-existing raw material the form of an object adapted to an end), something which in a sense *already exists*."[17]

Knowledge, Althusser says, is not the process of visually registering what comes in front of us; it is not a reflex, as Engel's vulgate of materialism pretended. Knowledge is the construction of an object:

> "We must completely reorganize the idea we have of knowledge, we must abandon the mirrors myths of immediate vision and reading, and conceive knowledge as a production [...] The invisible is defined by the visible as *its* invisible, *its* forbidden vision: the invisible is not therefore simply what is outside the visible (to return to the spatial metaphor), the outer darkness of exclusion—but the *inner darkness of exclusion*, inside the visible itself because defined by its structure."[18]

The structure of the visible is the determined form that cognitive production gives not only to its modes and properly epistemic contents, but also and precisely to the world that has been circumscribed and made visible by them. The metaphor of the visual field cutting out the visible world really allows us to grasp the issue of knowledge as production which is central to Althusser's theory.

To assert that knowledge needs to be understood as production is a statement rich with implications, not all of them developed by Althusser. The first is a merely gnoseological implication relative to the way the mind adapts to the world, making it become the "world of the mind."

> "It is therefore a question of producing, in the precise sense of the word, which seems to signify making manifest what is latent, but which really means transforming (in order to give a pre-existing raw material the form of an object adapted to an end), something which in a sense *already exists*, This production, in the double sense which gives the production operation the necessary form of a circle, is the *production of knowledge*."[19]

Here Althusser begins with Marx's refusal to confuse real objects and the objects of knowledge (a confusion that instead intentionally and explicitly dominates Hegel's theory).

The cognitive object is the result of a specific and determined activity of production. The 1857 *Introduction* to Marx's *Foundations of the Critique of Political Economy* (also known as *Grundrisse*) is the most important reference for anybody interested in understanding how the concept of knowledge as production works:

> "It seems to be correct to begin with the real and the concrete, with the real precondition, thus to begin, in economics, with e.g. the population, which is the foundation and the subject of the entire social act of production. However, on closer examination this proves false. The population is an abstraction if I leave out, for example, the classes of which it is composed. [...]. In

this way Hegel fell into the illusion of conceiving the real as the product of thought concentrating itself, probing its own depths, and unfolding itself out of itself, by itself, whereas the method of rising from the abstract to the concrete is only the way in which thought appropriates the concrete, reproduces it as the concrete in the mind. But this is by no means the process by which the concrete itself comes into being. [...]. Therefore, to the kind of consciousness—and this is characteristic of the philosophical consciousness—for which conceptual thinking is the real human being, and for which the conceptual world as such is thus the only reality, the movement of the categories appears as the real act of production—which only, unfortunately, receives a jolt from the outside—whose product is the world; and—but this is again a tautology—this is correct in so far as the concrete totality is a totality of thoughts, concrete in thought, in fact a product of thinking and comprehending; but not in any way a product of the concept which thinks and generates itself outside or above observation and conception; a product, rather, of the working-up of observation and conception into concepts. The totality as it appears in the head, as a totality of thoughts, is a product of a thinking head, which appropriates the world in the only way it can, a way different from the artistic, religious, practical and mental appropriation of this world. The real subject retains its autonomous existence outside the head just as before; namely as long as the head's conduct is merely speculative, merely theoretical. Hence, in the theoretical method, too, the subject, society, must always be kept in mind as the presupposition."[20]

Here, condensed in surprising words, we find a double overturning of perspectives.

First Marx asserts that the concrete is the product of an activity of abstraction. That is to say he asserts that what we conceive as concrete is nothing but the activity of thinking the concrete, and therefore an activity of the mind. At first glance this might appear to be an idealist way of reasoning. But this is not the case, since Marx is not talking of the relation between real and rational when he talks about the concrete and the mind. What Marx defines as concrete is the totality of the real as projection of mental activity. And what Marx calls a thinking mind is not the Kantian pure I, nor even the Hegelian Subject that becomes Spirit. The thinking mind Marx is talking about is that work which produces reality, that is to say work as projection.

At the same time, Marx adds that "the concrete subject" (historical data, material that is determined in the form of subject) remains firmly autonomous outside the mind.

The ontological priority of matter is not questioned by Marx here; he wants to say instead that matter, in its becoming (biological, historical, relational), produces a projective activity, an activity of thought secreting what we can call a concrete totality, that is to say a form of the world that does not pre-exist thinking productivity. The world is the psychodynamic intersection between all the infinite projective levels activated by mental activity in its social and historical determinations.

Althusser developed a theory that took the critique of historicism and the idealist claim for mental reproducibility of reality as its starting point. In this way, Althusser let us see something already implicit in Marx's text: that the world is first of all a produced world, the product of man's past labor as well as of past and present mental activity.

But there is another implication, only mentioned and not fully developed by Althusser, whose evident traces we nonetheless find most clearly in Marx's work, even in the same 1857 *Introduction.*

This second implication concerns the productive character of mental labor, that is to say the passage from the notion of abstract labor to that of *general intellect.*

What does "abstract labor" mean for Marx? With this expression Marx refers to labor simply as producer of exchange value, and therefore as pure distribution of time materialized in value. The fact that activity deployed in time produces objects possessing a concrete usage is not at all interesting from capital's point of view. Capital is not interested in the fact that the time invested in labor produces beautiful shoes or pots to cook potatoes. Capital is interested in producing an accumulation of capital through these objects. Capital is interested in the production of abstract value. To this purpose, capital doesn't need to mobilize specific and concrete abilities to create qualitatively useful objects, but an abstract distribution of time without quality.

> "Indifference towards any specific kind of labour presupposes a very developed totality of real kinds of labour, of which no single one is any longer predominant. As a rule, the most general abstractions arise only in the midst of the richest possible concrete development, where one thing appears as common to many, to all Then it ceases to be thinkable in a particular form alone. On the other side, this abstraction of labour as such is not merely the mental product of a concrete totality of labours. Indifference towards specific labours corresponds to a form of society in which individuals can with ease transfer from one labour to another, and where the specific kind is a matter of chance for them, hence of indifference."[21]

We talk about abstract labor when the workers give their time for producing value in conditions of complete indifference to the useful quality of their product.

The abstraction of labor, that is to say the transformation of human activities into empty performances of abstract time, is progressively expanding to all possible forms of social activity. The final point of this process is the subsumption of the productive labor of mental activity itself the sphere of value-production, which results in its ultimate reduction and abstraction.

This second implication present in Marx's *Grundrisse* (not only in the Introduction, but also in the section known as "*Fragment of machines*") becomes an essential element in the Workerist and Compositionist theories of the 1960s and 1970s. What finds its grounding here is the prefiguration of the most advanced tendencies in the current modes of capitalist production: the subsumption of mental labor within the productive process and the progressive reduction of mental labor to abstract labor, labor with no useful quality and no meaning, mental time serving only for the production of exchange value.

### *General intellect* and concrete totality in *Grundrisse*

In the 1960s, Critical Humanism (gravitating around the figures of Marcuse and Sartre) had found great energies in Marx's *Early Writings*. Human original authenticity was both the starting point and the teleological meaning of revolutionary engagement.

Althusser's structuralism is most of all an invitation to read *Capital*, since the structure of the productive process is considered the place where a critical comprehension both of the existing world and of the revolutionary process leading to its destruction is to be achieved.

Italian Neo-Marxist Workerism inspired by Compositionism shifts attention to the *Grundrisse*, Marx's work first published in Italy in 1968. Social composition and the formation of revolutionary subjectivity can be explained neither by the idealist hypostasis of a human nature to be realized through historical action nor by the analysis of the implicit contradiction in the structure of productive relations. Neither the presupposition of a humanity needing to be redeemed, nor the analysis of capital are sufficient to understand what happens on the scene of 20th-century history, on the stage of working class struggles and of capital's restructuring.

We need to adopt the point of view of labor in its most advanced manifestations, *it is necessary to assume the standpoint of the refusal to work*, in order to understand the dynamics both of productive transformation and of political revolt. When we do that, we can finally see that social composition is in constant transformation, altering the productive, technological, economic and political contexts. The motor of this constant transformation is the dynamic of subtraction of lived time from the wage-relation.

Compositionist theory positions itself in an anti-laborist perspective: the Italian Neo-Marxists gathered around the journal *Classe operaia* (*Working Class*) intended to study the constitution of autonomous collective activity, starting from the subtraction of lived time from labor, the refusal to work and the project of its extinction.

From the first page of *Capital*, Marx states that it is necessary to differentiate between generic activity, where humans relate to nature and the society of other humans, and a specific form of wage-earning labor, that is to say the lending of abstract time in exchange for a wage.

The refusal of work does not mean the erasure of activity, but the valorization of human activities which have escaped from labor's domination.

In *Capital*, Marx defines "abstract labor" in the following terms:

> "If then we disregard the use-value of commodities, only one property remains, that of being products of labour. But even the product of labour has already been transformed in our hands. If we make abstraction from its use-value, we abstract also from the material constituents and forms which make it a use-value. The useful character of the kinds of labour embodied in them also disappears; this in turn entails the disappearance of the different concrete forms of labour. They can no longer be distinguished, but are altogether reduced to the same kind of labour, human labour in the abstract."[22]

As an effect of capitalistic development, industrial labor loses any relation to the concrete character of activity, becoming purely rented out time, objectified in products whose concrete and useful quality does not have any interest other than that of enabling the exchange and the accumulation of plus-value.

> "Equality in the full sense between different kinds of labour can be arrived at only if we abstract from their real inequality, if we reduce them to the characteristic they have in common, that of being the expenditure of human labour-power, of human labour in the abstract."[23]

The industrial worker (and more generally, as a tendency, the entire cycle of social labor) is the bearer of a purely abstract and repetitive knowledge. Abstraction, this centripetal and at the same time unifying force traversing the modern period, reaches its perfection in the digital era. The labor of physical transformation of matter has become so abstract that it is now useless: machines can replace it completely. At the same time, the subsumption of mental labor has begun, and with it the reduction of mental labor itself to an abstracted activity.

> "Labour appears, rather, merely as a conscious organ, scattered among the individual living workers at numerous points of the mechanical system; subsumed under the total process of the machinery itself, as itself only a link of the system, whose unity exists not in the living workers, but rather in the living (active) machinery, which confronts his individual, insignificant doings as a mighty organism. In machinery, objectified labour confronts living labour within the labour process itself as the power which rules it; a power which, as the appropriation of living labour, is the form of capital."[24]

The worker appears overwhelmed, reduced to a passive appendage producing empty time, to a lifeless carcass. But then, immediately, the vision changes:

> "The increase of the productive force of labour and the greatest possible negation of necessary labour is the necessary tendency of capital, as we have seen. The transformation of the means of labour into machinery is the realization of this tendency. In machinery, objectified labour materially confronts living labour as a ruling power and as an active subsumption of the latter under itself, not only by appropriating it, but in the real

> production process itself; the relation of capital as value which appropriates value-creating activity is, in fixed capital existing as machinery, posited at the same time as the relation of the use value of capital to the use value of labour capacity; further, the value objectified in machinery appears as a presupposition against which the value-creating power of the individual labour capacity is an infinitesimal, vanishing magnitude."[25]

Thanks to the accumulation of science and the general forces of the social intellect, Marx repeats, labor becomes superfluous. Capital, in its purest form, tends to eliminate human labor in its immediate, material form as much as possible, in order to replace it with the technological use of science. The development of this trend virtually takes the productive global system out of the paradigmatic orbit of the modern capitalist system. A new paradigmatic system needs to be found, if we want to understand and, more importantly, liberate the new constellation of human activity, technologies, interfaces and social interactions. But a paradigmatic shift has a different timing from that of the technological and productive potentialities of *general intellect*. It gets tangled in the slow time of culture, social habits, constituted identities, power relations and the dominant economic order. Capitalism, as a cultural and epistemic, as well as economic and social, system, semiotizes the machinic potentialities of the post-industrial system according to reductive paradigmatic lines. The heritage of the modern period, with all its industrial clanking as well as with the clanking of its mental habits and of its aggressive and competitive imaginary, weighs on the development of new perspectives as an insurmountable obstacle preventing the deployment of a redistribution of wage-earning labor and its extension.

> "Capital here—quite unintentionally—reduces human labour, expenditure of energy, to a minimum. This will redound to the benefit of emancipated labour, and is the condition of its emancipation."[26]

The time of immediate labor becomes quantitatively irrelevant, if compared to an elaborate automated system. The reduction of necessary labor time and therefore the progressive elimination of workers, is seen by *Potere operaio* as a jolly perspective: in Compositionist discourse it translates into trusting the auto-assertive capacities of the intellect against its capitalistic use.

> "As soon as labour in the direct form has ceased to be the great well-spring of wealth, labour time ceases and must cease to be its measure, and hence exchange value [must cease to be the measure] of use value. *The surplus labour of the mass* has ceased to be the condition for the development of general wealth, just as the *non-labour of the few*, for the development of the general powers of the human head. With that, production based on exchange value breaks down, and the direct, material production process is stripped of the form of penury and antithesis. The free development of individualities, and hence not the reduction of necessary labour time so as to posit surplus labour, but rather the general reduction of the necessary labour of society to a minimum, which then corresponds to the artistic, scientific etc. development of the individuals in the time set free, and with the means created, for all of them."[27]

The alliance between technological power and general social knowledge meets the resistant power of the capitalist model, which dominates the social, cultural and psychological expectations of a proletarianized humanity.

The economy, like a general semiotic cage, forbids the development of the potential still existing in the material and intellectual structure of technology. Let's return to Marx:

> "Capital itself is the moving contradiction, [in] that it presses to reduce labour time to a minimum, while it posits labour time, on the other side, as sole measure and source of wealth. Hence it diminishes labour time in the necessary form so as to increase it in the superfluous form; hence posits the superfluous in growing measure as a condition—question of life or death—for the necessary. On the one side, then, it calls to life all the powers of science and of nature, as of social combination and of social intercourse, in order to make the creation of wealth independent (relatively) of the labour time employed on it. On the other side, it wants to use labour time as the measuring rod for the giant social forces thereby created, and to confine them within the limits required to maintain the already created value as value."[28]

These pages—read and valorized by the Compositionist theorists in the same years that the *Grundrisse* began to be known in Italy—define with incredible lucidity the direction taken by the development of 20th-century social, political and economical history.

The concept of *abstract labor* is the best possible introduction to an understanding of the digitalization of the productive process first made possible and finally generalized by the diffusion of microelectronics.

When Marx speaks of capital as a moving contradiction, he prefigures the astonishing history of the 20th century, when capital itself destroyed the potentialities it had created within the technical domain because of the instinct to conserve its social and economic model. When he foretells the development of creative, artistic and scientific faculties, Marx anticipates the intellectualization of labor nowadays characteristic of the post-fordist era.

At a certain point in the development of the application of intelligence to production, the capitalist model becomes a paradigmatic cage, constraining intelligence in the form of wages, discipline and dependence.

The concept of paradigm was not available to Marx, who found a surrogate for it with often ambiguous concepts of Hegelian derivation. The idea of a dialectical overcoming to be realized through negation, or the overturning and liberation of a hidden nucleus, is also derivation of the Hegelian conceptual system.

After the experience of the twentieth century, we understand very well that modern history does not proceed towards a positive exit along a dialectical path, and that there is no dialectical overcoming on the horizon. Capital seems rather to be a pathogenic mechanism, a sort of "double bind." Gregory Bateson[29] uses the concept of a double bind in order to understand a paradoxical form of communication, where the relational context is contradicted by the meaning of communication. Double binds are contradictory injunctions: for instance those orders, solicitations or requests where the enunciating subject asks the message addressee one thing with words and another, contradictory one, with gestures, affection and intonation. A double bind derives from juxtaposing two semiotic codes in a relational context or from the superposition of two different interpretive codes in the development of a unique process. On the historical level we can assert that capital semiotizes the technological process according to a code (that of economic valorization) that is inadequate to its material and social meaning. The social content of capitalist production contradicts its own semiotic framework. Therefore it produces a system of misunderstandings, contradictory injunctions and perverse juxtapositions.

Let's think of the so-called problem of unemployment, for instance. In reality, technological development tends to make manual labor useless and its evaluation in terms of wages impossible. But since the relational context where this message and this process are inserted is that of capitalism, which is founded on wage-earning regulations and labor's centrality, a double bind starts functioning.

The concept of a double bind has nothing to do with dialectics. Double binds are resolved only when the relational context is redefined, starting from the level of enunciation.

No total overturning is possible in the face of the capitalist double bind, since as a matter of fact there is no positive or negative totality in the social history of capitalism.

## Hans-Jürgen Krahl's theory: science, work and technique

Hans-Jürgen Krahl died in a car accident one night in 1970. Though not even thirty, he was one of the most influential thinkers of the anti-authoritarian German movement. The movement had exploded in the streets since 1967, when a young student aged 26, Behno Onesorg, was killed by the police during an anti-imperialist rally against the Persian Shah. After that other students rapidly joined the movement, fighting for the democratization of German society, protesting against the Vietnam War and denouncing, with astonishing actions of revolt, the mediatic overloading operated by the newspapers belonging to the Springer group.

From its origins, the German movement—then mainly organized along the lines of the SDS (*Sozialisticher Deutscher Studentbund*, German Socialist Student League)—was attracted by two different hypotheses: the "organizational" and the "spontaneous." In the following years the first would be grouped in the *Rote Zellen* [Red Cells] of Marxist-Leninist inspiration, the second in the multiform experiences of the youth movements, the *Jugendzentren* and the *Autonomen* collectives.

In the two years period before his death, Hans-Jürgen Krahl elaborated the general lines of a post-Leninist revolutionary theory. In his book *Konstitution und Klassenkampf*[30] (*Constitution and Class Struggle*) he questions the possibility of reducing the new social composition of intellectual labor to the political and organizational categories of the traditional workers' movements. His meditations start from the Frankfurt School theories, specifically Adorno's, developing them with respect to the praxis of industrial alienated labor and anti-authoritarian struggles. Krahl is rethinking the question of the relation between social composition and avant-garde political organization. Lenin answered the question in the subjectivist and voluntaristic way that was to dominate the revolutionary landscape of the century, but in the 1960s the movements had started looking for other solutions.

> "The traditional theories of class consciousness, especially the ones derived from Lenin, tend to separate class consciousness from its economic elements. They neglect the meta-economic, constitutive role played by productive subjectivity in the creation of wealth and civilization."[31]

The analytical separation between the levels of the economy and of consciousness had a legitimate grounding in a time when productive labor was structurally separated from intellectual labor, but it tends to lose its meaning once intellectual work has joined the process of general production in a constitutive way.

Production is not to be considered a merely economic process, ruled solely by the law of supply and demand; extra-economic factors have their role in that process and they are all the more relevant when the labor cycle is intellectualized. Social culture, divergent imaginations, expectations and disillusions, hatred and loneliness all modify the rhythm and the fluidity of the productive process. Emotional, ideological, and linguistic domains condition social productivity. This becomes clearer the more those same emotional, linguistic, and projective energies are involved in the process of value production.

Hans Jürgen Krahl succeeds in anticipating the innovative quality of the productive transformations characteristic of the last decades, the period that marks the exit from the industrial model. He anticipates this conceptually, following the abstract categories of critical Marxism.

> "Working time remains the measure of value even when it no longer includes the qualitative extension of production. Science and technology make possible the maximization of our labor capacity, transforming it into a social combination that, in the course of the capitalist development of machinery, increasingly becomes the main productive force."[32]

In his "Theses on the General Relation Between the Scientific Intelligentsia and Proletarian Class Consciousness," published in 1969, in the journal *Sozialistische Korrespondenz—Info*, Krahl focuses on the essential core of the movement's political problems.

Technology is the central issue, understood as the determined form of the relation between science and labor processes.

> "The technological translation of science into a system of mechanisms constituting a fixed capital—which has been systematically implemented since the end of the nineteenth century—and the tendency towards automation have changed what Marx called the real subsumption of labor under capital. The real subsumption is different from a purely formal one because it modifies qualitatively even the technological structure of the immediate labor process. This happens through the systematic application of the social forces of production and the separation between labor and science. The labor process then, understood as the organic exchange between man and nature, is socialized in itself. One of the most remarkable traits of the real subsumption of labor by capital is, as Marx said, 'the conscious application of science, which is a general product of social development, to the immediate process of production.' Social combination makes production increasingly scientific, thereby constituting it as a totality, as a 'total' worker, but at the same time reducing the working ability of the single individual to a simple moment."[33]

These analytical considerations necessarily led the young theoretician to postulate the decisive issue capable of radically questioning the organizational modalities and the political projects of the twentieth century workers' movement: the anti-authoritarian groups in the 1960s made them uncertain, but were not able to get rid of them.

> "The absence of a reflection about the theoretical construction of class consciousness as a non-empirical category [...]

had the consequence, within the socialist movement, of reducing the concept of class consciousness to its Leninist meaning, which is inadequate to the metropolis."[34]

Leninism, as a model of organization and way of understanding the relation between social consciousness and the general labor process is incapable of reading the metropolitan condition.

Leninism is based on the separation between the labor process and higher-level cognitive activities (that is to say consciousness). This separation is founded on proto-industrial work, since the workers have knowledge of their own abilities, but no awareness of the cognitive system structuring society. The roots of this separation become more and more fragile when the mass workers, forced into an increasingly parceled and alienating work activity, develop their sociality in a dimension that is immediately subversive and anti-capitalistic.

Finally this separation has no further grounding when we discuss the mental forms of social labor, since when each intellectualized operator is the vehicle of a specific form of knowledge, s/he perceives—although in a fragmented, confused and tormented manner—the social system of knowledge underlying the entire productive cycle.

**Digital Panlogism**

In those same years, Marcuse was also addressing the issue of the relation between forms of thought and forms of social production.

The productive finalization of technology ends up subjugating the thinking process from the standpoint of its own epistemological structures.

"The feature of operationalism—to make the concept synonymous with the corresponding set of operations—recurs in the linguistic tendency 'to consider the names of things as being indicative at the same time of their manner of functioning, and the names of properties and processes as symbolical of the apparatus used to detect or produce them'[4] This is technological reasoning, which tends "to identify things and their functions" [5]."[35]

Beginning with the idealistic frame pictured in works like *Reason and Revolution* and *Hegel's Ontology*, which proposed a tormented version of Hegelian thought focused on negativity, processuality and separation, Marcuse writes in his *One Dimensional Man*:

"The totalitarian universe of technological rationality is the latest transmutation of the idea of Reason."[36]

In *Eros and Civilization*, a book published in Italy in 1967, Marcuse develops a discourse on the liberatory potentialities represented by technology, while in *One Dimensional Man* he denounces the reduction of these same potentialities by functionalism. Marcuse opposed the dialectics of self-realizing reason to functionalist reductions. His position remains an idealistic one, and there is no concrete reference to social recomposition processes in his theory. He understands, nonetheless, an essential point of the late capitalist process: he sees the tendency towards a total integration of Logos and production through technology. At the horizon of the tendency described by Marcuse we find the digitalization of the world: digitalization as a paradoxical realization of Hegelian Panlogism in a non-dialectical, disempowered and pacified version:

> "The incessant dynamic of technical progress has become permeated with political content, and the Logos of technics has been made into the Logos of continued servitude. The liberating force of technology—the instrumentalization of things—turns into a fetter of liberation; the instrumentalization of man."[37]

The use of algorithms in the productive processes, and their transmission through logical devices, isolates an operational kind of rationality. But in this way the world is subsumed (overturning Hegel) in a digital and logical reduction, and therefore trapped forever in the capitalistic form embodied as technical Reason.

> "Technology has become the great vehicle of *reification*—reification in its most mature and effective form."[38]

We can say that the essential question for Hegelian theory is the reduction of reality to Logos and therefore the establishment of the Same, the abolition of every difference and the foundation of Identity. Throughout modern history we have witnessed a series of attempts to restore Identity either through violence or homologation, whether by democratic or totalitarian regimes. Romanticism tries to retrace the path leading to an origin where the premise of identity can be rediscovered. Twentieth-century totalitarianism stems from this obsession. The ethnic totalitarianism of Fascist states pretended to realize the Same on the basis of the myth of common roots, while the totalitarian Communist state pretended to realize the Same through the realization of the historical ideal of a society without differences.

But the reality of differences could not be vanquished. Even if reduced and oppressed they are always reborn in violent and resentful forms. In social life people are dominated on the contrary by inessential and egotistical claims, by nationalisms, regionalisms and racisms.

Identity, though, realizes itself on another level, that of Information. This level subsumes every space of the human habitat, replacing the historical perception of time with a digital one. The production of the Same is determined then as a program generating a succession of states that exclude the inessential by defining it.

From this point of view, computerized society can be understood as Panlogism realized.

Absolute Knowledge is materialized in the universe of intelligent machines. Totality is not History, but the virtual assemblage of the interconnections preprogrammed and predetermined by the universe of intelligent machines. Hegelian logic has thus been made true by computers, since today nothing is true if it is not registered by the universe of media machines. The totality generated by computers has replaced Hegel's totality.

We could even say that the global Net founds a Totality without Totalization.

The matrix is replacing the event. This is the final point of modern *Rationalisierung*.

To be recognized in the networked universe one must become compatible with the generative logic of the matrix. What does not belong to a codified domain is not socially recognizable or relevant, although it still exists in the domain of irrelevance, of residuality. It then reacts with rage and despair, in order to violently reassert its existence.

When History becomes the development of Absolute Computerized Knowledge difference is not vanquished, or resolved: it becomes residual, ineffectual, unrecognizable.

# 2

# The Soul at Work

### Digital labor and abstraction

Today, what does it mean to work? As a general tendency, work is performed according to the same physical patterns: we all sit in front of a screen and move our fingers across a keyboard. We type.

On the one hand, labor has become much more uniform from a physical and ergonomic point of view, but on the other it is becoming much more differentiated and specialized with respect to the contents that it develops. Architects, travel agents, software developers and attorneys share the same physical gestures, but they could never exchange jobs since each and every one of them develops a specific and local ability which cannot be transmitted to those who do not share the same curricular preparation and are not familiar with the same complex cognitive contents.

When labor had a substantially interchangeable and depersonalized character it was perceived as something foreign. It was mechanically imposed by a hierarchy, and represented an assigned task that was performed only in exchange for wages. The definition of dependent work and wage-earning was adequate for this kind of social activity, which consisted in the selling of one's time.

Digital technologies open a completely new perspective for labor. First of all they transform the relation between conceiving and executing, and therefore the relation between the intellectual contents of labor and its manual execution. Manual labor is generally executed by automatically programmed machinery, while innovative labor, the one that effectively produces value, is mental labor. The materials to be transformed are simulated by digital sequences. Productive labor (labor producing value) consists in enacting simulations later transferred to actual matter by computerized machines.

The content of labor becomes mental, while at the same time the limits of productive labor become uncertain. The notion of productivity itself becomes undefined: the relation between time and quantity of produced value is difficult to determine, since for a cognitive worker every hour is not the same from the standpoint of produced value.

The notion of abstraction and of abstract labor needs to be redefined. What does "abstract labor" mean in Marx's language? It means the distribution of value-producing time regardless of its quality, with no relation to the specific and concrete utility that the produced objects might have. Industrial labor was generally abstract since its specific quality and concrete utility was completely irrelevant compared to its function of economic valorization. Can we say that this abstract reduction is still active in the era of info-production? In a certain sense, yes, we can, and we can also say that this tendency is pushed to its extremes, since labor has lost any residual materiality and concreteness, and the productive activity only exerts its powers on what is left: symbolic abstractions, bytes and digits, the different information elaborated by productive activity. We can say that the digitalization of the labor process has made any labor the same from an ergonomic and physical point of view since we all do the same thing: we sit in front of a screen and we type on a keyboard. Our activity is later transformed by a concatenation of machines into an architectural project, a television script, a surgical operation, the moving of forty metal boxes or a restaurants' provisioning.

As we have already said, from a physical standpoint, there is no difference between the labor performance of a travel agent, a technician working for an oil company or a writer of detective stories.

But we can also say the opposite. Labor has become part of a mental process, an elaboration of signs rich with knowledge. It has become much more specific, much more specialized: attorneys and architects, computer technicians and mall vendors all sit in front of the same screen and type on the same keyboards: still, they could never trade places. The content of their elaborating activities is completely different and cannot be easily transmitted.

On the other hand, also from a physical point of view, chemical, metal and mechanical workers do completely different jobs, but it takes only a few days for a metal or mechanical worker to acquire the operative knowledge necessary to do the job of a worker in the chemical industry and vice versa. The more industrial labor is simplified, the more it becomes interchangeable.

Human terminals perform the same physical gestures in front of computers and they all connect to the universal machine of elaboration and communication: yet the more their jobs are physically simplified, the less interchangeable their knowledge, abilities and performance. Digital labor manipulates absolute abstract signs, but its recombining function is more specific the more personalized it gets, therefore ever less interchangeable. Consequently, *high tech* workers tend to consider labor as the most essential part in their lives, the most specific and personalized.

This is exactly the opposite of what happened with the industrial worker, for whom eight hours of wage labor were a sort of temporary death from which s/he could wake up only after the alarm bells rang, announcing the end of the working day.

**Enterprise and desire**

In its humanistic Renaissance meaning the word enterprise refers to an activity aimed at giving the world a human form. The "enterprise" of the humanistic artist enterprise is the sign of humanity's independence from fate and even divine will. For Machiavelli, enterprise is like politics in that it emancipates itself from fortune and realizes the republic, a space where different human wills test and compare their cunning and their ability to create.

In its capitalistic meaning, the word enterprise acquires new nuances, although it never loses its sense of free and constructive action. These new nuances all pertain to the opposition of labor and enterprise. Enterprise means invention and free will. Labor is repetition and executing action. Enterprise is an investment of capital generating new capital, thanks to the valorization that labor makes possible. Labor is a wage-earning service that valorizes capital but devalues workers. What is left today of the opposition between workers and enterprise, and how is the perception of the very notion of enterprise changing in the social imagination?

Enterprise and labor are less opposed in the social perception and in the cognitive workers' consciousness, that is to say the consciousness of those performing the highest level of productive labor and valorization and who represent the general tendency of labor's social processes. Those active in jobs with a high cognitive level, therefore those who could rarely trade their places, do not oppose their labor to the creation implied by the word enterprise: on the contrary, they tend to consider their labor, even if formally dependent, to be an enterprise where they can spend the best part of their energy, independently from the economic and juridical condition in which it expresses itself.

In order to understand this mutation in the perception of the notion of enterprise, we need to consider a decisive factor: while industrial workers invested mechanical energies in their wage-earning services according to a depersonalized model of repetition, *high tech* workers invest their specific competences, their creative, innovative and communicative energies in the labor process; that is, the best part of their intellectual capacities. As a consequence, enterprise (independently from the juridical relation between property and labor) tends to become the center towards which desire is focused, the object of an investment that is not only economical but also psychological. Only if we consider this can we understand why in the last two decades disaffection and absenteeism have become a marginal phenomenon, while they had been the central element in social relations during the late-industrial period.

In the 1980s (and even more, as we know, in the 1990s) the average labor time increased impressively. In the year 1996, the average worker invested in it 148 hours more than their colleagues did in 1973. According to the US Bureau of Labor Statistics the percentage of individuals working more than 49 hours per week grew from 13% in 1976 to 19% in 1998. As for managers, it grew from 40% to 45%. The prevision that the development of computerized technologies, favoring automation, would determine a reduction of social labor time proved both true and false, but in the final analysis we have to consider it false. It is true indeed that necessary labor time decreases in the sphere of industrial production, and therefore it is true that a growing number of industrial jobs are eliminated, replaced by machines or transferred to areas of the world where labor costs nothing and is not protected by unions. But it is also true that the time apparently freed by technology is in fact transformed into cyber time, a time of mental processing absorbed into the infinite production processes of cyberspace.

How is it possible to explain the workers' conversion from disaffection to acceptance? Certainly, one of the reasons is the political defeat suffered by the working class after the end of the 1970s because of the technological restructuration, the consequent unemployment and the violent repression inflicted on the political avant-garde. But this is not enough.

In order to understand the psycho-social change of attitude towards labor, it is necessary to consider a decisive cultural transformation linked to the shift of the social core from the domain of manual labor to that of cognitive labor.

What is happening in the domain of cognitive labor? Why does this new kind of worker value labor as the most interesting part of his or her life and therefore no longer opposes the prolongation of the working day but is actually ready to lengthen it out of personal choice and will?

To answer this question we need to consider several factors, some of which are difficult to analyze in this context. For instance in the last decades urban and social communities progressively lost their interest, as they were reduced to containers empty of humanity and joy in the relations they foster. Sexuality and conviviality have been transformed into standardized mechanisms, homologated and commodified: an anxious need for identity progressively replaced the singular pleasures of the body. Books like Mike Davis' *City of Quartz* and *Ecology of Fear* show that the quality of existence has affectively and psychologically deteriorated, due to the rarefaction of community ties and the sterilizing obsession with security.

It seems that ever less pleasure and reassurance can be found in human relations, in everyday life, in affectivity and communication. A consequence of this loss of eros in everyday life is the investment of desire in one's work, understood as the only place providing narcissist reinforcement to individuals used to perceiving the other according to rules of competition, that is to say as danger, impoverishment and limitation, rather than experience, pleasure and enrichment.

In the last decades, the effect produced in everyday life is that of a generalized loss of solidarity. The imperative of competition has become predominant at work, in media, in culture at large, through a systematic transformation of the other into a competitor and therefore an enemy.

**Wealth?**

But we still have not answered our question: how did it happen that after a long period of social autonomy marked by the refusal of work, when social solidarity prevailed over competition, and quality of life over power and the accumulation of money, labor has regained a central position in the imagination, both in the scale of socially recognized values and in the collective psychology? Why do such a large part of workers today consider work the most interesting part of their life, no longer opposing the lengthening of their working day and instead spontaneously choosing to increase it? Of course, this is also due to the dramatic worsening of social protections, determined by thirty years of *deregulation* and the elimination of public structures of assistance, but this is only a partial reason.

On an anthropological level a determinant aspect has been the assertion of a life model totally focused on the value of wealth, and the reduction of the concept of wealth to economic and purchasing power. But in fact, the identification of wealth with property is not at all self-evident.

To the question "What is wealth?" we can answer in two completely contrasting ways. We can evaluate wealth on the basis of the quantity of goods and values possessed, or we can evaluate wealth on the basis of the quality of joy and pleasure that our experiences are capable of producing in our feeling organisms. In the first case wealth is an objectified quantity, in the second it is a subjective quality of experience.

Money, bank accounts and economic growth are not the only things driving this new affection for labor dominating the psychological and economical scene of the last twenty years. But they are certainly a dominant factor. The economistic ideology is compulsively focused on the conviction that loving one's job means money, and that money means happiness. This is only partially true.

Let's repeat the question: what does wealth mean? The only answer available to this question is naturally an economic one: wealth means possessing the means that allow us to consume, namely the availability of money, credit and power. Yet this is still a poor answer, a partial, perhaps even completely wrong answer, producing misery for all, even for those capable of accumulating a lot of these things. This answer conceives wealth as a projection of time aimed at gaining power through acquisition and consumption. But one could instead conceive of wealth as the simple capacity to enjoy the world available in terms of time, concentration and freedom.

Naturally these two definitions of wealth are in conflict, and not only as definitions. They are indeed two different modalities of relation to the world, time, and the body. The more time we spend acquiring means for consumption, the less time we have to enjoy the world available to us. The more we invest our nervous energies in the acquisition of purchasing power, the less we can invest them in enjoying ourselves. It is around this issue—completely ignored by economic discourse—that the question of happiness and unhappiness in hyper-capitalistic societies is played out today. In order to have more economic power (more money, more credit) it is necessary to devote more and more time to socially homologated labor. This means though that it becomes necessary to reduce the time for joy and experience, in a word, for life. Wealth understood as enjoyment decreases proportionally to the growth of wealth understood as economic accumulation, for the simple reason that in the latter framework mental time is destined to accumulation rather than enjoyment.

On the other side, wealth understood as economic accumulation increases in proportion with the reduction of the dispersive pleasure, causing the social nervous system to suffer contraction and stress, without which there cannot be any accumulation.

But the two perspectives produce the same effect: the expansion of the economic domain coincides with a reduction of the erotic sphere. When things, bodies and signs become a part of the semiotic model of the economy, wealth can only be experienced in a mediated, reflected and postponed way. As in an infinite play of mirrors, what is really experienced is the production of scarcity and need, compensated by a fast, guilty and neurotic consumption because we can't waste time; we need to get back to work. Therefore wealth is no longer the ability to enjoy things, bodies and signs in time, but the accelerating and expansive production of their loss, transformed in exchange value and anxiety.

Now we can finally answer the question: how did it happen that work regained a central place in social affectivity and why did society develop a new affection for work?

One reason is well-known: in a situation of competition workers are obliged to accept this primordial blackmail: work as much as possible or die. But there is another answer we can give, concerning the impoverishment of everyday life and the relation to others, the loss of eroticism in the communicative experience.

The reasons behind the new love of working are to be found not only in a material impoverishment derived from the collapse of social warranties, but also in the impoverishment of existence and communication. We renew our affection for work because economic survival becomes more difficult and daily life becomes lonely and tedious: metropolitan life becomes so sad that we might as well sell it for money.

**Labor, communication, community**

The word "enterprise" that, in the industrial phase of capitalism, merely meant a capitalist organization with economical finalities, like the development of human labor and the accumulation of value, now means something infinitely more complex. Regaining something of its original humanistic meaning, the word enterprise refers to the responsible human initiative of transforming the world, nature and one's very relation with others.

Of course, the enterprise develops within the frame of the capitalist economy and therefore its limits are the same as those characterizing essential capitalist forms: exploitation, production of scarcity, violent imposition, and rules founded on force. But there is an ambiguity that needs to be understood: enterprise is subdued to capitalist rule, the two are not at all the same thing. The desperate attempt to find freedom, humanity and happiness where the accumulation of value reigns rests on this potential difference.

The investment in desire comes into play at work, since social production has started to incorporate more and more sections of mental activity and of symbolic, communicative and affective action. What is involved in the cognitive labor process is indeed what belongs more essentially to human beings: productive activity is not undertaken in view of the physical transformation of matter but communication, the creation of mental states, of feelings, and imagination.

Classical industrial labor and specifically the organized form of the Fordist factory had no relation with pleasure. It had no relation with communication either: communication was actually thwarted, fragmented and obstructed as long as workers were active in front of the assembly line. Industrial labor was characterized mainly by boredom and pain, as is witnessed in metallurgist and mechanics' reports to sociologists who, in the 1950s and 1960s, studied the workers' conditions of alienation and atomization.

Therefore industrial workers found a place for socialization in subversive working communities, political organizations or unions where members organized against capital. Workers' communism became the main form of good life and of conscious organization for the class that capital forced (and still forces) to live a great part of its existence in inhuman conditions. Communism was also the only form of knowledge for the class that capital forced (and still forces) to live in conditions of mental passivity. Communism was the form of universal consciousness produced by the working community. In the communist organization workers could leave their conditions of abstract labor to rediscover concrete communication through a common project, a shared mythology. This kind of communism has nothing to do with the historical communism imposed throughout the twentieth-century by feudal, military and ideological bureaucracies. The only relation between the State Communism imposed by the Leninist parties in the Soviet Union and elsewhere, and the autonomous communism of the workers, is the violence systematically exerted by the first over the second, in order to subdue, discipline and destroy it.

Political communism was the power of backward and despotic bureaucracies that exercized repression and violence in order to protect their own power from the globalizing dynamics of capital. Once these same dynamics became stronger than the bureaucracies' resistance, political communism was finally defeated by world capitalism and the economic power of capitalist globalization. The autonomous communism of the workers underwent a different destiny: parallel, to a certain extent, but still different. Workers' communism has been partially subsumed by capital, by transforming workers' opposition into innovative dynamics (refusal of work, substitution of workers' labor with machines, and the production shift towards digital cycles).

Partially, then, workers' communism has been reduced to a sterile residue, always more marginal. There is no more workers' communism, since workers no longer belong to a community. Industrial workers have not disappeared from the face of the earth. Globalization, in fact, greatly enlarged the cycle of industrial labor, moving it to the poorest peripheries of the planet and degrading it to a condition of semi-slavery.

But capital's deterritorialization has taken place rapidly, infinitely more rapid than the time required for workers to build their communities. Paul Virilio describes very well the function of velocity in the relation between states and military blocs throughout the modern period. But the velocity of class struggle, the war between working class and capital, was even more decisive. Digital technology and the financial character of the world economy have accelerated the pace of capital transfers, of changes in the organization of work and the creation and dismantling of productive centers all around the world. This acceleration obstructs the formation of communities in the places where capital starts the productive process.

While industrial labor did not imply communication and did not attract desiring energies, the opposite can be said for cognitive labor. Info-workers can sometimes be described as craftsmen, since they invest their knowledge and creativity in the process of producing networks. Their energy is displaced from one point of the productive network to the other: capturing fragments of information in order to recombine them within a constantly changing general frame.

The investment of desire, which for the craftsman deeply connected to its local community and its needs used to have a reassuring character, for the info-worker develops along very different lines, producing anxiety, incertitude and constant change. Flexibility is the necessity to displace, move, and constantly change perspectives. This is the double-sided fulcrum of desire and productivity for the info-worker. Experience, knowledge and flux are at the same time the constitutive aspects of existence and the context of active labor.

Cognitive labor is essentially a labor of communication, that is to say communication put to work. From a certain point of view, this could be seen as an enrichment of experience. But it is also (and this is generally the rule) an impoverishment, since communication loses its character of gratuitous, pleasurable and erotic contact, becoming an economic necessity, a joyless fiction.

Moreover, not all forms of work that could somehow be defined as mental activities are linked to communication, invention and creation. A characteristic aspect of info-labor is the fact that it cannot be reduced to any category, not even to deterritorialization or to autonomy or creativity. The people who sit at their terminals in front of a screen, repeating every day the same operation a thousand times, relate to their labor in a way similar to industrial workers. What we need to understand, though, is the new element, the fact that creative labor in the network circle is infinitely flexible, it can be assembled and disassembled, and that it is precisely in this dismantling identification that we can find both its desire and its anxiety. Within mental labor as a whole we need distinguish properly cognitive labor, where intellectual energies are engaged in a constant creative deterritorialization, and mental labor of a purely applicative kind, which is still prevalent quantitatively. Even within the mental labor cycle, we can distinguish *brain workers* from *chain workers*. But I'll focus on the most innovative and specific forms, since they represent the trend that is transforming the whole of social production.

**Cognitive labor in the network**

In order to understand the transformation that social perception of labor underwent during the past few decades and how it determined the workers' condition of cultural and psychological dependence, we need to analyze both the investments of desire within the domain of info production and the formal aspects of labor relations.

The digital transformation started two different but integrated processes. The first is the capture of work inside the network, that is to say the coordination of different labor fragments in a unique flow of information and production made possible by digital infrastructures. The second is the dissemination of the labor process into a multitude of productive islands formally autonomous, but actually coordinated and ultimately dependent. As we have said, cognitive labor manifests itself as info labor, that is to say as the infinite recombination of myriad information, available through a digital support. When cooperation means transferring, elaborating and decoding digitalized information, it is evident that the network works as its natural frame.

The function of command is no longer a hierarchical imposition, localized in the factory, but a transversal, deterritorialized function, permeating every fragment of labor time.

The non-hierarchical character of network communication becomes dominant in the entire cycle of social labor. This contributes to the representation of info-labor as an independent form of work. But this independence, as we have seen, is in fact an ideological fiction, covering a new and growing form of dependency, although no longer in the previous formal hierarchies, whose command over the productive action was direct and voluntary. This new dependency is increasingly apparent in the automatic fluidity of the network: we have a strict interdependence of subjective fragments, all distinct but objectively dependent from a fluid process, from a chain of automatisms both external and internal to the labor process which regulate every gesture, every productive parcel.

Both simple executing workers and entrepreneurial managers share the vivid perception that they depend on a constant flow that cannot be interrupted and from which they cannot step back save at the price of being marginalized. Control over the labor process is no longer guaranteed by the hierarchy of bigger and smaller bosses typical of the Taylorist factory, but it is incorporated in the flux. Cellular phones are probably the technological devices that best illustrate this kind of network dependency. The cellular phone is left on by the great majority of info-workers even when they are not working. It has a major function in the organization of labor as self-enterprise that is formally autonomous but substantially dependent. The digital network is the sphere where the spatial and temporal globalization of labor is made possible. Global labor is the endless recombination of a myriad of fragments that produce, elaborate, distribute and decode signs and informational units of all sorts. Labor is the cellular activity where the network activates an endless recombination. Cellular phones are the instruments making this recombination possible. Every info-worker has the capacity to elaborate a specific semiotic segment that must meet and match innumerable other semiotic fragments in order to compose the frame of a combinatory entity that is info-commodity, Semiocapital.

But for this combination to become possible, a single, infinitely flexible (and constantly reactive to the calls of Semiocapital) productive segment is not enough: a device is needed, capable of connecting the single segments, constantly coordinating and localizing in real time the fragments of info production. Cellular phones, the most important article of consumption of the last decade, provide this very function at a mass level. Industrial workers had to spend eight hours daily in a specific place if they wanted to receive their wage in exchange for productive gestures performed again and again in a specific territory.

The mobility of the product was made possible by the assembly line while workers had to remain motionless in space and time. Info-workers, instead, constantly move all along the length, breadth and depth of cyberspace. They move to find signs, to elaborate experience, or simply to follow the paths of their existence. But at every moment and place they are reachable and can be called back to perform a productive function that will be reinserted into the global cycle of production. In a certain sense, cellular phones realize the dream of capital: that of absorbing every possible atom of time at the exact moment the productive cycle needs it. In this way, workers offer their entire day to capital and are paid only for the moments when their time is made cellular. Info-producers can be seen as neuro-workers. They prepare their nervous system as an active receiving terminal for as much time as possible. The entire lived day becomes subject to a semiotic activation which becomes directly productive only when necessary.

But what emotional, psychological, and existential price does the constant stress of our permanent cognitive electrocution imply?

**The factory of unhappiness**

Happiness is not a matter of science, but of ideology. This is how it should be addressed.

Even if in the public discourse it is not possible to pursue a scientifically based and coherent discourse on happiness, we see entire flows of communication built on the idea of happiness. We witness the circulation of fragmentary and imaginary solicitations which are rarely justified or coherent, yet remain extremely effective. In the 1990s, while the productive process was becoming immaterial, the dominant rhetoric was all focused on happiness: to be happy is not only possible, but almost mandatory. In order to reach this goal, we have to follow certain rules and modes of behavior.

Both the totalitarian and the democratic political discourse have placed happiness on the horizon of collective action. Totalitarianism imposed mandatory behavior procedures and asked of its citizens to accept them enthusiastically, lest they be marginalized and persecuted: s/he who's unhappy is a bad patriot and a bad communist, s/he is a saboteur, and so on and so forth.

Democracy does not expect an enthusiastic consent. On the contrary, in a mature vision we conceive democracy as an endless pursuit of a possible *modus vivendi* allowing individuals to identify with personal and public behaviors capable of capturing some relative happiness.

Capitalism is often (and with no reason) presented as the inseparable companion of democracy (while we know that instead it often prospers in the shadow of far from democratic regimes), but in fact it is not tolerant at all, since it expects enthusiastic participation in a universal competition where it is impossible to win without fully and convincingly deploying all of our energies.

Totalitarian regimes, like Nazism, Fascism and the authoritarian Socialist states, denied freedom to their people in the name of a collective and homologated happiness, thereby producing an infinite sadness.

But even the liberal economy, with the cult of profit and success represented in a caricatured but persuasive manner in advertising discourse, ended up producing an unhappiness caused by constant competition, defeat and guilt.

In the 1990s the *New Economy*'s ideology asserted that free market play creates a maximum of happiness for humanity in general. In fact, one of *New Economy*'s effects was the assimilation of ideological and advertising messages, and the transformation of advertising into a sort of paradigm of economic theory and political action.

It is well known that the discourse of advertising is based on the creation of imaginary models of happiness that consumers are invited to replicate. Advertising is a systematic production of illusions, and therefore of disillusions, as well as of competition and defeat, euphoria and depression. The communicative mechanism of advertising is based on the production of a sense of inadequacy coupled with the solicitation to become a consumer, in order to feel adequate and to finally realize the happiness that has been eluding us.

### Self-realization and the refusal of work

As we have already seen, in the 1960s and 1970s, at the very peak of the industrial system's mature phase, when the Fordist mechanical and repetition based model realized its perfection, the workers' feeling of estrangement from industrial labor and their refusal to work, found support in a cultural wave that placed the issue of alienation at the core of its critical system. In its philosophical meaning, alienation meant a loss of human authenticity, the exchange of what in men and women is more essentially human for something materially valuable, such as a salary, money, or consumption goods. Philosophies of idealist stripe, influenced by Existentialism, were widely circulated in the political movements of those years. They considered capitalism the reason for an alienation that takes away people's humanity in exchange for a subaltern and conformist participation in the circuit of goods. As a consequence, these philosophies indicated as their major political objective the achievement of a social condition where productive labor and self-realization would come together.

Then in the 1970s feminist and gay movements identified with the idea that "the personal is political." They meant that it was not only political power and the government of the republic that was at stake in the social struggle. What was at stake was first of all the quality of life, pleasure and pain, self-realization and respect for diversity: desire as the engine of collective action.

*A/traverso* (*In-between*), a journal which held a certain influence on the youth movements of the 1970s, came out once with the title "The practice of happiness is subversive when it becomes collective." The 1977 movement—in its colorful and creative Italian version and in its British one as well, which was punk, gothic and disturbing—was founded on one intuition: desire is the determining field for every social mutational process, every transformation of the imagination, every shift of collective energy. It is only as a manifestation of desire that we can understand the workers' refusal of the wage relation, of conforming their lives to the timing of the assembly line realized through absenteeism and sabotage.

Rich, aware, productively and culturally autonomous, liberated individualities deviated with rage from the ideology of sacrifice and the work ethic: work was denounced as a pure hierarchical repetition, deprived of any intelligence or creativity. That 1977 movement therefore used the ideology of happiness as a powerful critical instrument against the Taylorist factory and the Fordist productive cycle, but also against the social and disciplinary structure based on the factory model.

In the following years some decisive events completely upset the productive, social and cultural landscape.

First of all, digital technology spread very quickly, transforming in many ways the modalities of productive labor and its concatenations.

Secondly, the hierarchical structure of the factory model collapsed.

The aspiration to self-realization became fundamental in the reconstruction of a functioning social model perfectly fitting digital productive modalities. Social history can be seen as the uninterrupted story of the refusal of work and the reconstructions of the productive system, where reciprocal resistance and reaction coexist. In industrial societies capital and the working class had contradictory interests, but they also had a common interest. Contradiction came from the fact that capital aimed to take from living labor the greatest possible amount of labor time and value, while the workers' interest was instead that of avoiding exploitation, saving their physical and intellectual energies for themselves. At the same time though, workers and capital both had an interest in reducing necessary labor time, introducing productive automatisms, machines and technologies. This is what actually happened. The workers' struggle for power pushed capital to use machines instead of workers, exactly as Karl Marx had anticipated in his *Grundrisse*. The introduction of microelectronic technologies, the digitalization of machinery and the computerization of productive processes led rapidly to a transformation of the characteristics of labor and to its general intellectualization.

During the twentieth-century the issue of the relation between intellectual and manual labor was constantly raised. Max Weber thematizes this relation, Lenin uses it as a basis for the theory of the party and Gramsci rethinks it under a new light. But when intellectual labor is mentioned in the theoretical tradition of the working movement, it refers to a function that is separated from the productive process of commodities, as a function of control that governs and ideologically organizes consent and therefore an executive and political function.

The properly productive function was essentially delegated to manual labor, that is to say to the direct transformation of physical materials. Intellectual labor gained material power, becoming the instrument of the political and technical empowering of industrial labor and of the working class. Automation had already started spreading during the mature industrial period: it implied that machinery could assume transformational functions, so that manual labor was greatly strengthened. In the 1970s, more and more operative functions were transferred to machines, with the introduction of numerically controlled instruments and flexible automation systems. But the decisive transformation of the 1980s was the systematic computerization of working processes. Thanks to digitalization, every concrete event not only can be symbolized, but also simulated, replaced by information. Consequently it becomes possible to progressively reduce the entire production process to the elaboration and exchange of information.

And in fact, what is information? It is not simply a transfer of signs, referring to an object or an event. Information is a creation of form, which is inoculated into the object or the event. It is the creation of value, the production of goods. Every object, event, and commodity can be replaced by algorithmic information capable of transforming that object or that event into exchangeable existence.

Info-production reached all cycles of goods production, services, material and semiotic objects, since digitalization created a simulacrum of the world operationally integrated to the physical world.

The formation of the info-productive model was accompanied by a cultural and psychic evolution in the labor force, substantially changing the very perception of activity. In classic industrial society, workers felt expropriated of their intellectuality, individuality and creativity. In high tech production cognitive faculties are in fact put to work, and personal peculiarities seem to be valorized.

The intellectualization of labor, a major effect of the technologic and organizational transformation of the productive process in the last two decades of the twentieth-century, opens completely new perspectives for self-realization. But it also opens a field of completely new energies to the valorization of capital. The workers' disaffection for industrial labor, based on a critique of hierarchy and repetition, took energies away from capital, towards the end of the 1970s. All desires were located outside capital, attracting forces that were distancing themselves from its domination. The exact opposite happened in the new info-productive reality of the *new economy*: desire called new energies towards the enterprise and self-realization through work. No desire, no vitality seems to exist anymore outside the economic enterprise, outside productive labor and business. Capital was able to renew its psychic, ideological and economic energy, specifically thanks to the absorption of creativity, desire, and individualistic, libertarian drives for self-realization.

**Prozac-economy**

In the 1990s, the decade of the alliance between cognitive labor and a reconstituting capital, financial flows generated by *net trading*, the advertising cycle, venture capital and retirement funds moved to the cycle of virtual production. Cognitive labor could therefore become enterprise, entering the formation circuits of the Techno-Sphere and media-scape. Armies of creative engineers, of libertarian programmers and artists became the proletarians of intelligence, people who owned nothing but their cognitive labor force and who could start an enterprise on an economic and creative basis. In those years a veritable battle took place, between a diffuse, libertarian, equalitarian and collective intelligence and the *new economy*'s oligopolies.

The diffusion of the dot.com enterprise also represented a redistribution of social revenue, conquering revenue for research and experimenting. The model of the network, the principle of productive collaboration and *open source* took roots in society thanks to the alliance between recombining capital and cognitive labor.

The alliance of the 1990s happened under the sign of a neo-liberalist ideology that glorified the market, describing it as a space capable of perfect self-regulation. Perfect self-regulation, of course, is a naïve fairytale since real economic play involves power relations, violence, the mafia, theft and lies. Thus monopolies came to dominate information technologies, the media system and all those other sectors where cognitive workers had invested their energies in the illusion of being able to constitute independent enterprises. The alliance between cognitive labor and recombinatory capital ended with the submission of the market to oligopolistic domination, and cognitive labor was subjected to the decisions of the big financial groups dominating the world economy. In the year 2000, the stock exchange collapse determined a loss of energy in the innovative sectors, and restored the domination of the old oil-based economy, redirecting the world towards the meaningless horror of war.

Competition has been the universal belief of the last neo-liberalist decades. In order to stimulate competition, a powerful injection of aggressive energy became necessary, a sort of permanent electrocution producing a constant mobilization of psychic energies. The 1990s were the decade of psycho-pharmacology: a Prozac-economy.

Frenetic rhythms dominated mid-1990s finance, consumption and lifestyles, producing the effect of the systematic use of euphoria-inducing drugs, including neuro-programming substances. A growing part of Western societies, subjected to an uninterrupted mental hyper-excitation to the point of collapse, evoked as in an exorcism the urban legend of the *millennium bug*. Once that phantasmatic threat dissolved, the real collapse came. But the *new economy*'s collective psyche had already reached its point of no return. When in 1999 Alan Greenspan spoke of the "irrational exuberance of the market," his words were more of a clinical than a financial diagnosis. Exuberance was an effect of the drugs and of the over-exploitation of available mental energy, of a saturation of attention leading people to the limits of panic.

Panic is the anticipation of a depressive breakdown, of mental confusion and disactivation.

And finally the moment of the Prozac crash came.

The beginning of the new millennium had glorified megafusions: AOL and Time Warner united their tentacles in order to diffusely infiltrate the global mind. Immediately after, the European telecommunication enterprises invested huge amounts of money into UMTS (Universal Mobile Telecommunications System). These were the last actions before the crash involving Worldcom, Enron, and entire sectors of the net-economy. This crisis, which was only a faint anticipation of the 2008 final catastrophe, was the first manifestation of the breakdown suffered by swarms of cognitive workers more and more affected by psychopathological syndromes and stress.

**Panic depressive syndrome and competition**

In his book *La Fatigue d'être soi*, Alain Ehrenberg discusses depression as a social pathological syndrome, specifically depending on situations characterized by competition.

"Depression begins to develop after the disciplinary behavioral models and the rules of authority and conformity to the prohibitions that assigned a destiny to social classes and gender collapsed faced with the new norms pushing each and everyone to individual action, forcing individuals to become themselves. Because of this new norm, the responsibility of our lives is now fully assigned to each of us. Depression then manifests itself as pathology of responsibility, dominated by the feeling of inadequateness. The depressed individuals are not up to the task, they are tired of having to become themselves."[1]

Depression is deeply connected to the ideology of self-realization and the happiness imperative. On the other side, depression is a way to define through the language of psychology a behavior that was certainly not considered pathological outside of competitive, productive and individualist contexts.

"Depression is part of a field of problems, dominated more by inhibition, slackening and asthenia than by moral pain: the ancient 'sad passion' is transformed into a block of action, and this happens in a context where individual initiative becomes the measure of the person."[2]

Competition implies a risky narcissistic stimulation, because in a highly competitive context, like that of a capitalistic economy and specifically of the *new economy*, many are called but only a few are chosen. Social norms do not acknowledge the possibility of failure, since this failure would be assigned to a psycho-pathologic context. There is no competition without failure and defeat, but the social norm cannot acknowledge the norm of failure without questioning its own ideological fundaments, and even its own economic efficiency.

The other side of the *new economy* is naturally the use of psycho-stimulant or anti-depressive substances. This is a hidden, negated, removed side, but absolutely decisive. How many, among *new economy* operators, survive without Prozac, Zoloft or even cocaine?

Dependence on psychotropic substances, those one can buy at the pharmacy and those one can buy on the street, is a structural element of the psychopathologic economy.

When economic competition is the dominant psychological imperative of the social consortium, we can be positive that the conditions for mass depression will be produced. This is in fact happening under our eyes.

Social psychologists have in fact remarked that two pathologies are of great actuality in these last decades of liberalist hyper-capitalism: panic and depression.

Panic is a syndrome psychologists don't understand very well, since it seems to have occurred only rarely in the past. Panic syndrome has been only recently diagnosed as a specific phenomenon, and it is hard to find its physical and psychic reasons, but it is even harder to find an adequately effective therapy against it. I don't have the ambition to offer any solution to the pathologic problem this syndrome poses. I'm just making some observations on the meaning of panic. Panic is the feeling we have when, faced with the infinity of nature, we feel overwhelmed, unable to receive in our consciousness the infinite stimulus that the world produces in us. The etymology derives from the Greek word *pan*, that means "everything existing": the god named Pan appeared bringing a sublime, devastating folly overtaking those who received his visit (see James Hillmann's *An Essay on Pan*). But then how can we explain the diffusion of this kind of syndrome in our time? Is it possible to find any relation between it and the context in which it manifests and spreads?

The social context is a competitive society where all energies are mobilized in order to prevail on the other. Survival is no longer based on reaching a position of sufficient preparation and abilities, but it is constantly questioned: if one does not win, one can be eliminated, in a few days or a few months.

The technological context is the constant acceleration of the rhythms of the global machine, a constant expansion of cyberspace in the face of the individual brain's limited capacities of elaboration.

The communicational context is that of an endless expansion of the Infosphere, which contains all the signals from which competition and survival depend.

Isn't this a very similar situation to the one pictured by the Greek etymology of the word panic?

The infinite vastness of the Infosphere is superior to the human capacities of elaboration, as much as a sublime nature overcomes the capacities of feeling that the Greeks could summon when faced with the god Pan. The infinite velocity of the expansion of cyberspace, the infinite velocity of exposure to signs perceived as vital to the survival of the organism produce a perceptive, cognitive and psychic stress culminating in a dangerous acceleration of all vital functions, such as breathing and heart beat, leading to collapse.

If there is anything meaningful in this interpretation of panic, then this is not simply an individual psychopathology, but an individual manifestation of a widely spread, quasi-generalized social syndrome. It is collective behavior that shows the most evident signs of panic.

Collective panic generates phenomena such as irrational aggressiveness against immigrants, senseless mass violence in stadiums, as well as other, apparently normal behaviors, like those characterizing personal relations in the contemporary urban space. These behaviors cannot be corrected with the instruments of political persuasion or judicial repression, because they have nothing to do with politics and ideology but depend on a social psychopathology induced by the Infosphere's excess, by the hyperstimulation and the endless cognitive stress affecting the social organism and caused by permanent electrocution.

Permanent electrocution is the normal condition of a system where network communicative technologies are used in a competitive social situation, projecting the organism in an infinite, hyper-fast flow of economically relevant signs.

Once the organism gets overtaxed to an unbearable degree, a panic crisis may lead to collapse, or the organism might detach itself from the flow of communication, manifesting a sudden psychic loss of motivation called depression by psychologists.

With depression we are affected first of all by a disinvestment of the energy previously used in a narcissistic way. Once the organism realizes that it is unable to sustain further competitive tension, that it is a loser in the relation that was absorbing all of its motivations, what takes place is a sort of zero degree of the exchange relation between the conscious organism and its world.

With depression we are always affected by a process of de-motivation, originated by the loss of an object that used to be the focus of narcissistic attention for the subject.

"The world doesn't make sense anymore"—says the depressed—since the object of his or her narcissistic passion is lost. This might explain the diffusion of depression as a secondary pathologic syndrome (if compared to the primary one, which I believe to be panic), in a society based on the principle of competition and supplied with the technological instruments necessary for the infinite acceleration of the communication circles surrounding the organism.

The description of these two complementary syndromes can be useful in order to address the psycho-social framework constantly generating and feeding the psychopathology of the present.

The aggressive young people addicted to amphetamines, riding in super-accessorized cars and going to work ready to give their best to increase their share in corporate earnings and to obtain their bosses' approval are all in the waiting room of panic. In the same way their younger skinhead brothers beat each other up every Sunday in the soccer stadium, expressing a form of panic accumulated weekly during their normal working week.

Political culture refuses to acknowledge that the legal drugs one can buy at the pharmacy, a source of astonishing profits for Roche and Glaxo, as well as the illegal ones, a source of profit for the mafia, are an essential factor (and in fact the most important one) of competitive society.

**Virtual class and cognitariat**

Virtual is a reality whose tangible physicality has been eliminated. Frigid Thought can well be recognized in the network world, where the relation to the other is artificially euphoric but substantially desexualized as well.

Frigid Thought is the a-critic exaltation of digital technologies. Digital technologies are based on the loss of the physicality of the world, on simulating algorithms capable of reproducing all life forms, except for only one quality: their tangible reality, their physical form and therefore their caducity.

Noah grouped in his ark all the creatures of the earth, in order to save them from the flood. Today in a similar way we can enter our air-conditioned arks and float on the waves of the digital deluge without losing contact with the cultural patrimony accumulated by humanity, keeping linked to the other arks, while at the same time, on the physical planet down there, barbarian hordes swarm and make war.

Those who can, isolate themselves in a pressurized and hyper-connected capsule. They are physically removed from other human beings (whose existence becomes a factor of insecurity), though ubiquitous, virtually present in any possible place according to their desires.

This schizophrenic geography needs indeed two different catalogues, two atlases describing supposedly separate worlds. The catalogue of the virtual class is sterilized. It proposes objects whose temporality and physicality have constitutively been removed. The removal of corporeality is a guarantee of endless happiness, but naturally a frigid and false one, because it ignores, or rather removes, corporeality: not only that of others, but even one's own, negating mental labor, sexuality and mental mortality.

It is because of these considerations that I see the need for a new notion, able to analyze the virtual class in corporeal, historical and social terms.

The notion of virtual class stresses the socially undefined, elusive character of the work flows produced by Semiocapital. The virtual class is the class of those who do not identify with any class, since they are not socially or materially structured: their definition depends on the removal of their own social corporeality.

This seems to me an interesting and useful notion. But I'd like to find a complementary concept, capable of defining the (denied) carnality and the (avoided) sociality of the mental labor at work in the production of Semiocapital. Therefore I use the notion of the cognitariat. The cognitariat is the semiotic labor flow, socially spread and fragmented, as seen from the standpoint of its social corporeality. The virtual class has no needs, but the cognitariat does. The virtual class is not affected by the psychic stress determined by the constant exploitation of attention. The cognitariat is affected. The virtual class cannot produce any conscious collective process except as collective Intellect. The cognitariat can identify itself as a conscious community.

It is evident that the word "cognitariat" includes two concepts: cognitive labor and proletariat.

Cognitariat is the social corporeality of cognitive labor. What is at stake within the social definition of cognitive labor is precisely the body, sexuality, mortal physicality, the unconscious.

In his most famous book, entitled *Collective Intelligence* (Perseus, 1999), Pierre Lévy proposes the notion of collective intellect. Thanks to the digital network, he writes, the idea of a collaborative participation of all human intellects to the creation of a collective intellect takes a concrete shape, and the creation of the world within technological, digital and virtual conditions becomes possible. But the social existence of cognitive workers does not exhaust itself with the intellect: cognitive workers, in their concrete existence, are bodies whose nerves become tense with constant attention and effort while their eyes are strained in the fixed contemplation of a screen.

# 3

## The Poisoned Soul

**From incommunicability to over-communication**

In the critical language of the 1960s, the word "alienation" was usually combined with the word "incommunicability." Beginning with these two words and almost half a century later, I will start conducting my analysis of the mutations in the socio-cultural and psychological landscape.

In the 1960s, industrial urban landscapes represented the background for a feeling of silent uneasiness and the rarefying of relational acts among human beings. Workers were forced to stand by the assembly line surrounded by a hellish metallic clanking noise: it was impossible for individuals to exchange a word, since the only comprehensible language was that of the machine. Thus the language of things took the place of the symbolic exchange. Space for communication seemed to fade away, while "the thing" entered every affective, linguistic and symbolic interstice.

These aspects of relational discomfort are well expressed by the literature of the industrial era that in the 1960s revealed itself with the *nouveau roman*, or Michelangelo Antonioni's cinema. In the post-industrial landscape of Semiocapitalism, relational discomfort is still a central element of the social scene, but it is the product of a completely different, even opposite, situation from the one characterizing the decade of full industrial development.

The present emerging uneasiness originates from a situation of communication overload, since we the assembly line, once linking workers through the movements of a mechanical apparatus, have been replaced by the digital telecommunications network, which links people through symbols. Productive life is overloaded with symbols that not only have an operational value, but also an affective, emotional, imperative or dissuasive one. These signs cannot work without unleashing chains of interpretation, decoding, and conscious responses. The constant mobilization of attention is essential to the productive function: the energies engaged by the productive system are essentially creative, affective and communicational.

Each producer of semiotic flows is also a consumer of them, and each user is part of the productive process: all exits are also an entry, and every receiver is also a transmitter.

We can have access to the modalities of digital telecommunication from everywhere and at all times, and in fact we have to, since this is the only way to participate in the labor market. We can reach every point in the world but, more importantly, we can be reached from any point in the world. Under these conditions *privacy* and its possibilities are abolished, if we understand this word in its fullest meaning and not only according to its specific juridical definition. Whe we use the word *privacy* we normally refer to a space sheltered from the public eye, that is to say to the very possibility of performing acts and exchanges that are purely private, not transparent. Juridical rules are constantly devised in order to protect citizens' privacy, forgetting that privacy represents not only the right not to be watched, but also the right to refuse to watch and to be continually exposed to watching and hearing what we would rather not see or hear. Advertising constantly violates this *privacy*, introducing its visual and auditory messages in every inch of our visual space, and in every second of our time. The diffusion of screens in public spaces (railway stations, airports, city streets and squares) is an integral part of this abusive occupation of the public space and the private dimension of our sensibility.

Everywhere, attention is under siege.

Not silence but uninterrupted noise, not Antonioni's *red desert*, but a cognitive space overloaded with nervous incentives to act: this is the alienation of our times.

The notion of alienation (to be other than oneself) can be configured in different forms. In the industrial domain it manifests itself as reification. We can then understand it according to the Hegelian concept of "by itself," which indicates a loss of authenticity but also the dialectical condition of a negation leading to the restoration of the entire being of the Subject, since—let's not forget this—for Hegel "Being is the Subject" as full deployment of the dialectic of the Absolute Spirit.

In the young Marx's analysis that humanistic socialism referred to, the concept of alienation is linked to the critique of commodity-centered fetishism, and of the alienating process of "becoming thing" experienced by workers and consumers. The overcoming of alienation in this context is understood as the rise of new subjects— the intact human beings of communism—freed from the commodities' domination and owners of their own working process.

Within the postindustrial domain, we should talk of de-realization, rather than reification. The concept of alienation is then understood as: 1) a specific psychopathological category; 2) a painful division of the self; 3) a feeling of anguish and frustration related to the inaccessible body of the other, to the dis-tonic feelings of a non-sympathetic organism incapable of living a happy relation with otherness and therefore with itself.

It is the third meaning of the term alienation that best describes our present times: an era marked by the submission of the soul, in which animated, creative, linguistic, emotional corporeality is subsumed and incorporated by the production of value.

The first two meanings defined the phenomenology of the malaise typical of the industrial sphere, where we can observe an effect of reification: the effect of "the self becoming thing." Within the social conditions of industrialism and industrial consumerism, individuals perceived their bodies as something of which they have been expropriated, something foreign.

In the third meaning, which describes the phenomenology of the malaise typical of the domain of immaterial labor, we can see an effect of de-realization: the social, linguistic, psychic, emotional impossibility of touching the thing, of having a body, of enjoying the presence of the other as tangible and physical extension.

The word "reification" refers to the "becoming thing" of human time, the loss of animation derived from the separation of mental and working functions, and the fact that the inanimate body depends on the thing. The word "de-realization" refers instead to difficulties experienced by the animated body in reaching the animated body of the other: a pathogenic separation between cognitive functions and material sociality.

## In the desert of language

The words "alienation" and "incommunicability" were so often quoted by the critical European discourse of the 1960s, that they became almost the epitome for that epoch, as much as the words "globalization" and "virtuality" can be considered the epitome of present times. Beyond any critical generalization and the anti-humanistic philosophical liquidation of the entire field of concepts connected to the word "alienation," it is necessary to rediscover the meaning and the historicity of these concepts in order to understand how they helped interpret that cultural "conjuncture," and how they could help us understand the new (is it really a new one?) human condition of connective times.

In his 1964 movie *Red Desert*, Antonioni captured the energies coming from figurative art and the *nouveau roman* to represent—through background colors, pop-style flat interiors and desolate industrial exteriors—a quality of experience where the warmth and immediacy of human relations were lost. Marriage crises, escape and adventure are simply occasions to describe a general condition of malaise inhabiting every relationship, and first of all the relation with the self. This was the crisis that the Italian *bourgeoisie* was experiencing in those years: it prepared the atmosphere leading to the 1968 revolt, a moment of liberation in which the new warmth of the collective replaced the coldness of private relations. Antonioni was the director who best succeeded at representing a passage that is not simply related to culture and politics, but first of all to the sensibility and quality of emotions. Being close to the experience of *pop art*, Antonioni could express, in color and form, the flattening of nuances and the industrial homologation of different aspects of existence.

This happens in a similar way in *Persona*, a 1966 film by Ingmar Bergman whose intentions were, however, completely different. In this extremely slow, dazzling black and white movie, the rarefying of communication becomes the stylistic cipher of the human ambience that was brewing in those years: later the new winds of warmth and eroticism brought by the students' revolt would finally change that entire emotional landscape. Silence and aphasia in *Persona* can't be understood as mere signs of individual psychopathologies, representing instead a historically and socially located incommunicability. Bergman's silence and the sunny sites of the Northern seaside resort where the action takes place are the metaphors for an emptiness that becomes loneliness, for the unbridgeable distance between bodies.

The concept of "alienation" was at the core of the critical discourse related to these two movies, extremely significant for the artistic scene of that decade. In that context, alienation referred to the submission of the person to the thing.

At the peak of the industrial age the world of things was exploding: serial production generated infinite exemplars of standardized objects, and the assembly line as a productive technique subjugated human gestures to mechanical rhythms. The machine thus became an animated object while the body was turned into an inanimate one, separated from any form of consciousness. At the same time mass consumption serialized behaviors in relation to existing merchandises.

Decades of serial reification influenced our perception to such an extent that today we are no longer capable of realizing up to which point the otherness of the thing transformed the world of every day experience, making us estranged from ourselves, if however we admit that "ourselves" means anything at all.

## The Serpent's Egg

In a 1977 movie entitled *The Serpent's Egg*, Ingmar Bergman tells the story of the rise of Nazism in 1920s Germany as if it were a (physical) poisoning of a (psychological) social space, an infiltration of the milieu of relations and everyday life. Bergman, who often treated the theme of alienation as psychological suffering, painful silence of the soul and incommunicability, proposed here a materialistic, almost chemical, explanation of the human degradation processes caused by Nazism.

In this movie, alienation has nothing to do with human essence: it is a consequence of the toxic substance penetrating and poisoning the air that the characters (Liv Ullmann and David Carradine) breathe inside their tiny habitation.

*The Serpent's Egg* is not considered one of the Swedish director's best films, yet in my opinion it is one of the most interesting ones from the perspective of his personal evolution and of the late-modern cultural process. This film opens the way to a new definition of historicity, understood as a psychological and linguistic process and thereby redefining alienation as a material, chemical, or rather neuro-chemical mutation. Social pathologies are first of all a communicational disorder. The critical notion of incommunicability marks a complex field of problems: the rarefaction of exchanges, uneasiness in affective relations, and the actual pollution of the human interaction field.

With *The Serpent's Egg* Bergman thinks anew the very question of incommunicability: communication between Ullmann and Carradine is progressively poisoned, since a toxic substance penetrates their roots, lungs, and finally their brains. Thus (in a crowd scene filmed in a slow, hypnotic motion) the social body is transformed by Nazism into an amorphous mass, deprived of its own will and ready to be led. The metaphor of psychological submission that we find in this movie is pertinent far beyond the example of German Nazism: it can characterize other processes of collective mental pollution, such as consumerism, television commercials, the production of aggressive behaviors, religious fundamentalisms and competitive conformism.

The metaphor of *The Serpent's Egg* avoids the essentialist and idealist definitions of the word that were prevalent during the 1960s, years marked by the *Hegelian Renaissance*. This metaphor has to be understood instead as the intuition of a psychological pathology spreading on a social scale. The explicative utility of the notion of alienation emerges once we extricate it from its properly Hegelian context. We can use it again, though, within a phenomenological and psychopathological context, in order to define the current scene in our own postindustrial times, when work-related disturbances tend to immediately involve the domain of language and emotions, of relations and communication.

In that 1977 movie, Bergman talked about what was then the future but today, in the new millennium, is already the present. The poison has been brought daily into our homes, like a nerve gas, acting on our psychology, sensibility, and language: it is embodied by television, advertising, endless info-productive stimulation, and the competitive mobilization of the energies. Liberal economics produced mutational effects in the organism: they are deeper than those produced by Nazism, since they are active within the biological and cognitive texture of society, in its chemical composition, and not on superficial forms of behavior.

That same year, on December 25, Charlie Chaplin died, the man with the derby hat, who told the story of the dehumanization of modern industrialism from the point of view of a humanity still capable of being human. There is no more room for kindness. *Saturday Night Fever* came out in movie theatres that fall, introducing a new working class, happily willing to be exploited during the entire week, in order to excel in dancing with greased hair on Saturday nights.

1977 is a turning point in the history of humanity; it is the year when a post-human perspective takes shape. 1977 is a year charged with ominous signals: in Japan it is the year of youth suicides—784. An enormous scandal is provoked by a chain of infantile suicides, thirteen in the month of October alone, among elementary school children. The generation born in the 1980s is destined to be the first video-electronic generation, the first generation to be educated in a milieu where mediatization prevails over any other form of relation with the human body. In the aesthetic and cultural styles of the following decades we witness a cleansing, disembodying process. It is the beginning of a long process of cultural sterilization, whose effects transform the first video-electronic generation into object and subject at once. The *clean* replaces the dusty, while the bold prevails over the hairy. During the following decade the epidemic danger of AIDS re-semiotizes the entire field of corporeality. Carnal contact is heavy with danger and electricity, becomes either rigid, frozen, or hyper hot in a pathological way. Thus is prepared the cognitive mutation of the last two decades of the twentieth-century. The organism becomes sensitive to the code and predisposed to connections, permanently interfacing with the digital universe.

Sensibility—not reason—perceived this mutation, and reacted with a self-destructive movement of craziness, whose most evident signal was the wide spreading of heroin addiction. The existential and artistic experience of the American no wave, of London punk and the Italian and German autonomous movements, signaled a last reawakening of consciousness, against the mutations occurring in the domain of the sensible and in collective psychology, against this pollution of the soul and the consequent de-animation of the body.

## Alienation and desire

The soul we have been discussing is a metaphor for the energy that transforms biological matter into an animated body. In a sense we could say that the soul is the relation to the other, it is attraction, conflict, relationship. The soul is language as the construction of the relationship with alterity, a game of seduction, submission, domination and rebellion.

In the history of capitalism the body was disciplined and put to work while the soul was left on hold, unoccupied and neglected. What the workers wished to do with their souls, their thoughts, language and affects presented no interest for the capitalist of the industrial times. Eight hours a day (or nine, ten, twelve) the body is forced to repeat strange, alienated, hostile movements. The soul is mute until it rebels; then the body refuses to submit, interrupting its services, breaking the chain and blocking the productive flow.

The alienation of the soul from the body was seen as the greatest disgrace by idealist humanism, yet it can finally appear as a form of power. Once alienation becomes active estrangement, the animated body recognizes its distance from capital interests. Then human beings rediscover their intellectual and psychological integrity, refusing to submit to wage labor and beginning the foundation of a community that is aware and free, cohesive and erotic.

The overturning of the body's submission to domination became possible precisely because the soul remained separate from it: language, relations, thoughts, all cognitive activities and affective faculties remained distant from the labor process and therefore they were free, despite the body's enslavement. Assembly-line workers, while forced to repeat the same movements, still had brains that thought freely, at least until their energies were available and fatigue and sadness did not prevail. Despite the machines' clanking, it was possible to discuss and start processes of autonomy and revolt. But in Semiocapitalism, the soul itself is put to work. This is the essential point of the postindustrial transformation that we experienced in the last decades of the twentieth-century.

While this transformation was taking place, philosophical thought changed the terms of the question. The word alienation disappeared from the philosophical lexicon beginning in the 1970s, and the historicist humanistic context where that word had acquired its meaning also disappeared. Post-structuralist theory has cast the question of alterity within new conceptual parameters. Notions like "desire," "discipline," "control" and "biopolitics" have replaced Hegelian and Marxist analytic notions. The question of power formations and independent social subjectivity was posed in completely new terms.

In the following pages I will analyze these themes, beginning with a meditation on some questions posed by authors who theorized the desiring and disciplined body at the end of the twentieth-century: in particular, I will focus on Michel Foucault, Gilles Deleuze and Félix Guattari, in addition to Jean François Lyotard.

But I will also cite another name, someone who had a very different perspective on things within that changing context, and focused on concepts such as "simulation," "implosion" and "catastrophe": I mean Jean Baudrillard, who was openly polemical towards philosophical positions predicated on desire. In those years, that debate remained marginal within the philosophical arena, but today we can see that its core is dense with meaning and full of theoretical and political implications which are still stunningly timely.

### Desire is an illusion

Buddhism devalues desire since it is the source of *maya*, the illusion flowing in the form of the world. Even the stoics understood that the major purpose of philosophical action is to cut our dependence from the flow of emotions and desires.

We certainly respect the superior wisdom capable of withdrawing from the flux of *maya*, suspending the addiction to passions' domination. The flowing of desire is a source of illusion, and the final goal of knowledge is the interruption of such flows. Yet we need to acknowledge that this very illusion is history, the city, falling in love, existence: it is the game we have been playing knowing it was a game. While trying to escape from the flux of *maya* we also try to understand it, to make some sense of it in our path to wisdom.

Yet it's not enough to acknowledge that wordly experience is the emanation of a psychic flow whose source is the mind, as it is not enough to understand that social reality is a point of psychodynamic intersection for innumerable mental drifts. Even once we have deeply understood this truth, we still need to come to terms with the effects of the illusion, whose name is reality.

Simplistic readings of Deleuze's and Guattari's theories have often misunderstood the notion of desire. In Deleuzian language and in its interpretation by the "desiring movement," as we can define it, desire is often perceived as if it were subjective, a force that would be positive *per se*.

I have to admit that on this point ambiguities can be found in the work of both philosophers. As I have to admit that in my own work of "political translation" of Deleuze's and Guattari's theories I have sometimes identified desire as a positive force opposing domination. But this form of vulgarization needs to be corrected.

Desire is not a force but a field. It is the field where an intense struggle takes place, or better an entangled network of different and conflicting forces. Desire is not a good boy, nor the positive force of history. Desire is the psychological field where imaginary flows, ideologies and economic interests are constantly clashing. To give an example, there is a Nazi form of desire.

The field of desire is central in history, since within such a field forces that are crucial for the formation of the collective mind, and therefore for the main axes of social progress, meet through juxtaposition and conflict.

Desire judges History, but who judges desire?

Ever since the corporations specializing in "imagineering" (Walt Disney, Murdoch, Mediaset, Microsoft, Glaxo) took control of the desiring field, violence and ignorance have been unleashed, digging the immaterial trenches of techno-slavery and mass conformism. These forces have colonized the field of desire. This is why the new cultural movements, like media-activism, emphasize the need of effective action in the constitution of the desiring field.

**Limit, alterity, re-composition**

We can think of the other as a limit, or we can think of it in terms of (com)passion.

*Anti-Oedipus* reminds us: *je est un autre*, "I is an other," revealing that the question of the other cannot be posed in merely social terms, as relation of the individual with the individuals around him. Alterity is the pulsional, phantasmatic, imaginary flow which displaces and transforms the very existence of subjectivity. Alterity is the productive Unconscious. What is produced by the Unconscious is a singular existence in its complex relation with the world.

The question of the limit, though, does not appear in Deleuze's and Guattari's texts.

In Hegelian language the limit is understood as "alienation": the other is the limit of the self, its diminishment and impoverishment. In a dialectic context alienation is the subject's limitation in its relation to the other, or the perception of the other as limitation. The Hegelian dialectic attributes to the historical process the task and the possibility of overcoming the limit, and of realizing a totalization where alterity is finally removed. But for us the limit is not a reduction of potency. The relation to otherness is constitutive of both psychological and social dynamics. It is structured through instable forms, for reasons that change throughout history. What has to be understood and analyzed is the way this relation has changed while we went beyond modernity.

We have seen already that the Workerist (Compositionist) critique of the dialectic abandoned the notion of alienation in favor of an idea of positive estrangement. In the context of Workerist and Compositionist theories, otherness is indeed acknowledged as a limit, but also as the condition for an expansion of the power of the self. The limit is a condition for potency: this is the meaning of the recomposition process. Social recomposition is the process through which the relation to the other is linguistically, affectively, and politically elaborated, then transformed into a conscious collective, an autonomous aggregate, a group in fusion, constructive in its rebellion. Beginning with the awareness that the other is the limitation of the existing organism, Italian Compositionist Workerism asserted that this limitation does not involve a loss, an impoverishment: it opens instead the possibility of collective experience, based on conflict. The limit (which is not reducible to any historical synthesis) cannot be exhausted: this also means that the pleasure of enjoying the other, who is at once limit and extension, cannot be exhausted.

In this way, once the field of dialectic materialism and historicism was abandoned, it began to be clear that the science of social transformation is much closer to the chemistry of gases than to the mechanics of sociology. There are no compact forces, unitary subjects that promote unequivocal wills. In fact there is no will: only flows of imagination, depressions of the collective mood, sudden illuminations.

There are abstract devices able to connect flows: valves, faucets, mixers that cut, stir and combine flows and events.

There is no subject opposing other subjects, but the transversal flows of imagination, technology, desire: they can produce vision or concealment, collective happiness or depression, wealth or misery.

On the other hand, the historical process is not a homogenous field where homogenous subjectivities are opposed, or where clearly identifiable projects would be conflicting. It is rather a heterogeneous becoming where different segments are active: technologic automation, panic psychosis, international financial circuits and identitarian or competitive obsessions. These heterogeneous segments neither sum up nor oppose each other: they enter concatenating relations that Guattari called "machinic arrangements" (*agencements*).

At the beginning of the known history of Western thought, Democritus proposed a philosophical vision of a "compositionist" kind. There is no object, no existent, and no person: only aggregates, temporary atomic compositions, figures that the human eye perceives as stable but that are indeed mutational, transient, frayed, and indefinable.

> "Being is in his [Democritus'] eyes an infinite multiplicity of masses, which are invisible because they are so small. They move in vacuum. When they come into contact, they do not make a unity, but by these meetings, uniting, they produce generation, and by separating they produce corruption."[1]

The history of modern chemistry on one hand, and the most recent cognitive theories on the other, confirm this hypothesis.

The shape of every object is the shape projected by the eye and the brain.

A person's being is the temporary fixation of a relational becoming in which people define themselves, for a moment or for their entire life, always playing with an imponderable matter.

Towards the end of the history of Western thought (at the exact point where it starts coming out from itself), Deleuze and Guattari open the way to a new philosophy that we could name Molecular Creativism. In their philosophical landscape the image of the body without organs plays an important role.

Let's consider the concept of a body without organs from a Compositionist point of view.

A body without organs is the process of reciprocal crossing between everything and everyone, the endless molecular flows from a composite body into another.

It is an orchid continuing to exist as a baboon, a bee, a rock, and a cloud.

It is not "becoming," Félix Guattari says, but multiple "becomings."

A body without organs is the atemporal, extended substance that becomes temporal in its "becomings," and becomes temporarily singular as an effect of chaosmotic creation, emerging from chaos in order to give shape to an enunciation, a collective intentionality, a movement, a paradigm, a world.

Guattari's notion of "*Chaosmosis*" describes this surfacing as concatenations of sense within chaos:

> "I is an other, a multiplicity of others, embodied at the intersection of partial components of enunciation, breaching on all sides individuated identity and the organized body. The cursor of chaosmosis never stops oscillating between these diverse enunciative nuclei—not in order to totalize them, synthesize them in a transcendent self, but in spite of everything, to make a world of them."[2]

The events of the planet appear like stormy and incomprehensible clouds. The history of late modernity appears like a chaos whose evolutional lines are unforeseeable. But what is chaos? Chaos is a form of the world that is too complex to be grasped by the limited categories available to humans.

More sophisticated sensors are necessary in order to understand extremely complex phenomena and even more complex categories, interpreting processes that seem fortuitous. Now an algorithm of a superior order is necessary. A chaosmotic concept, Deleuze and Guattari would say, since chaosmosis refers to the process of surfacing from what appears like a chaos of a conceptual, formal and paradigmatic order.

> "A concept is a set of inseparable variations that is produced or constructed on a plane of immanence insofar as the latter crosscuts the chaotic variability and gives it consistency (reality) a concept is therefore a chaotic state par excellence; it

refers back to a chaos rendered consistent, become Thought, mental chaosmos."³

The encounter between Italian Autonomous theory (Compositionist Workerism) and French desiring theory (Molecular Creativism) was not a fortuitous hazard, due to political and biographical vicissitudes. At a certain point, in the middle of social struggle, the autonomous movement necessarily had to use categories of a schizoanalytic kind, in order to analyze the process of formation of the social imaginary.

In the same way, in the middle of a psychoanalytic practice, Guattari had to use categories of a socio-critical kind, in order to analyze the process of psychogenesis, as Guattari himself explains in his book *Psychanalise et transversalité* [Psychoanalysis and Transversality], published in Italian with the title *Una tomba per Edipo. Psicoanalisi e transversalità* [A Tomb for Oedipus: Psychoanalysis and Transversality].⁴

The methods of Autonomist theory and Schizoanalysis coincide in their Compositionist method: they both reject any constituted subjective primacy, looking instead for the processes of transversal formation of those unstable, varying, temporary, singular aggregates that are called subjectivities down to their molecular dimension. Subjectivity does not pre-exist the process of its own production. In order to explain the process of social recomposition we need to refer to the notions of desire, machinic unconscious and schizoanalysis.

How can it be explained that—in a certain decade—workers all over the world started singing the same song? It was the visible manifestation of a complex phenomenon, like the formation of storms over the oceans. In order to understand the muscular relaxation of its entire neurovegetative system experienced by Western humanity in the 1960s, we need to understand what made it possible: which substances, languor, expectations, and sensations. Social insurgence is the manifestation of an extremely complicated architecture entered by the psychological, imaginary, and material flows structuring everyday experience.

**Depression and chaosmosis**

At the same time we need to explain how it happened that, at a certain point, sadness prevailed, and the fragile collective architecture of happiness collapsed.

> "Among the fogs and miasmas which obscure our *fin de millénaire*, the question of subjectivity is now returning as a leitmotiv. It is not a natural given any more than air or water. How do we produce it, capture it, enrich it, and permanently reinvent it in a way that renders it compatible with Universes of mutant value? How do we work for its liberation, that is, for its re-singularization?"[5]

This is the question asked by Félix Guattari on the last page of his last book, which was published in 1992 just before his death on an August night that same year.

The book he wrote previously, together with his accomplice and friend Gilles Deleuze, was titled *Qu'est-ce que la philosophie? (What is Philosophy?)* and had been published in 1991.

Many are the common topics of these two books, but the most important are the themes of chaos and old age: two subjects deeply connected, as we'll see. We can read in the conclusion to *What is Philosophy?*:

> "We require just a little order to protect us from chaos. Nothing is more distressing than a thought that escapes itself, than ideas that fly off, that disappear hardly formed, already eroded by forgetfulness."[6]

The question "what is chaos?" is thus answered in the following paragraphs:

> "They are infinite speeds that blend into the immobility of the colorless and silent nothingness they traverse, without nature or thought."[7]

There is chaos when the world starts spinning too fast for our mind to appreciate its forms and meaning. There is chaos once the flows are too intense for our capacity to elaborate emotionally. Overwhelmed by this velocity, the mind drifts towards panic, the uncontrolled subversion of psychic energies premise to a depressive deactivation.

In their introduction to *What is Philosophy?*, this fantastic and touching book written on the verge of an abyss, Deleuze and Guattari wrote that the moment had come for thinking of old age. Old age opens the doors to a chaosmotic wisdom capable of elaborating the infinite velocity of flows with the necessary slowness.

Chaos "chaotizes," and infinitely decomposes any consistence: the question of philosophy is to build levels of consistence without losing the infinity from where thinking emerges. The chaos we are talking about has an existence that is at once mental and physical.

> "Not only objective disconnections and disintegrations but an immense weariness results in sensations, which have now become woolly, letting escape the elements and vibrations it

finds increasingly difficult to contract. Old age is this very weariness: then, there is either a fall into mental chaos outside of the plane of composition or a falling-back on ready-made opinions."[8]

Chaos is too complex an environment to be deciphered by the schemes of interpretation we have at our disposal. It is an environment where the circulating flows are too fast for the mind to elaborate them. Subjectivity or rather the process of subjectivation is constantly measuring itself against chaos. Subjectivity constitutes itself precisely in this constant relation to an infinite velocity, from which the conscious organism derives the condition for the creation of a *cosmos* and of a provisory order, variable and singular. But subjectivity does not side with order, since this would paralyze it. Chaos is an enemy, but also an ally.

"It is as if the *struggle against chaos* does not take place without an affinity with the enemy."[9]

How is it possible to elaborate the infinite velocity of flows without being affected by the disaggregating effect of panic? Concepts, artistic forms, and friendship are the transformers of velocity allowing us to slowly elaborate what is infinitely fast without losing its infinite complexity, without having to recall the common places of opinion, communication, and redundancy.

The process of subjectivation creates simple semiotic, artistic, emotional and political concatenations through which chaosmosis becomes possible. For instance, art creates semiotic devices capable of translating the infinite velocity of reality flows into the slow rhythm of sensibility. Deleuze and Guattari define these sensible translators as "chaoids."

"Art is not chaos but a composition of chaos that yields the vision or sensation, so that it constitutes, as Joyce says, a chaosmos, a composed chaos—neither foreseen nor preconceived. Art transforms chaotic variability into *chaoid* variety [...] Art struggles with chaos but it does so in order to render it sensory."[10]

The process of *becoming-subject* is not at all natural: it happens within social, economic and media conditions that are constantly changing.

**The world's decrepitude**

*Chaosmosis* and *What is philosophy?* came out at the beginning of the 1990s: they were the years of passage beyond twentieth-century modernity, and represent an epoch of dissolution for the happy community. They also saw the formation of a new productive system where all architectures of solidarity vanished, the working-class community was eliminated by technical innovation, labor became precarious, and the collective intellect underwent a process of submission that has ambiguous, hardly decipherable, characteristics.

In those years Guattari proposed again the question of becoming subjects. Modernity built chaoids: political reducers of complexity, semiotic translators of sensibility, conceptual transformers. In their aging years, our two friends discovered the dissolution of modern chaoids, and perceived the resurfacing of chaos. Was their own old age related perhaps to the aging of the world?

Demography confirms it: old age is the destiny of our planet. The demographic curve has slowed down. Fifty years ago demographers anticipated that the earth would be populated by twelve billion people; we know today that we won't go beyond the nine billion mark. Births are decreasing in all cultural areas, with the exception of the Islamic world.

Tuned to the old age of the world, we can see our two cartographers of chaos facing the dissolution of meaning.

The years following 1989—after the sudden hope of a period of world peace, and the equally unexpected new apparition of war— were years of dramatic, painful, obscure changes. Yugoslavia's massacres were looming on the horizon, while the Soviet Union's collapse announced the reemergence of nationalism, later embodied by Putin's figure. Islamic integralism and fanaticism started to assert itself as political identity for a decisive sector of the excluded of the Earth. After the Rio De Janeiro Summit, where the President of the United States, Mr. Bush senior, declared the impossibility of negotiating on the lifestyle of American citizens, ecological disaster appeared as our common perspective.

In those years, Félix Guattari recorded the accumulating signals of barbarization, the re-emergence of fascism and the violence that capitalism brought with its victories.

The trajectory of conceptual creation was changing, it fragmented and recomposed itself following new directions, often losing sight of the horizon, losing its meaning and recognizable forms.

Depression. We don't find such a word in Guattari's texts: it is left in the margins, as if it were an incompatible topic for the creationist energy that animated his work, his research and his existence. If we pay careful attention to the last chapter of their last collective book, Gilles and Félix are in fact analyzing depression, confusion and dark horizons: the emergence of chaos.

**Aesthetic of the refrain**

*Chaosmosis* is the beginning of a meditation that Guattari left us to develop on the creation of a peculiar *cosmos*, that is to say, on a desiring energy endlessly reconstituting itself beyond depression, across and beyond the dark (but also enlightening) experience of depression.

There is a truth within depression. And in fact, as we have read, "it is as if the *struggle against chaos* did not take place without an affinity with the enemy." Depression is the vision of the abyss represented by the absence of meaning. Poetic and conceptual creativity, like political creativity, are the ways of chaosmotic creation, the construction of bridges over the absence of meaning. Friendship makes the existence of bridges possible: friendship, love, sharing, and revolt. *Chaosmosis* is a book attempting to traverse chaos through cosmic and creative bridges, practices (aesthetics, philosophy, schizoanalysis, politics) that could make possible the singularization of chaos, that is to say the isolation of a specific bridge over the endless and infinitely fast flow of things.

> "Infinite speeds are loaded with finite speeds, with a conversion of the virtual into the possible, of the reversible into irreversible, of the deferred into difference."[11]

Philosophy is the creation of concepts, and concepts are chaoids capable of isolating a singular cosmos, the modality of projective subjectivation. Art is instead the singular composition of chaos through the elaboration of forms, gestures, and environments assuming a concrete presence in the space of communication, vision, and projection.

With the expression "aesthetic paradigm," Guattari refers to the privileged position that sensibility has gained in present times, when productive and communicative relations lose their materiality and trace their trajectories in the space of sensible projections. Aesthetics is the discipline through which the organism and its environment become attuned. The tuning process is disturbed by the acceleration of infospheric stimuli and by semiotic inflation, the saturation of every space of attention and consciousness. Art registers and signals this disturbance, but at the same time it looks for new possible modalities of becoming, and aesthetics seems to be at the same time a diagnostic of the psychospheric pollution and a therapy for the relation between the organism and its world.

Guattari establishes a privileged relation between aesthetic and psychotherapeutic dimensions. The question of the relation between chaotic velocity and the singularity of lived time becomes decisive. In order to grasp temporal flows, the mind needs to build its own temporalities: these singular temporalities are *refrains* that make orientation possible. The notion of refrain leads us to the core of the schizoanalytic vision: the refrain is the singular temporality, the niche for individualizing the self where the creation of cosmos becomes possible.

Philosophy, art and schizoanalysis are practices of singular chaosmotic creation, that is to say they allow the configurations constituting the map of an existence to emerge from the infinite flux, like refrains. But these refrains can solidify and morph into semiotic, ritual, sexual, ethnic, and political obsessions.

On the one hand, the refrain protects the subject from the chaos of the *Infosphere* and the semiotic flows that carry him away like stormy winds. This is how, protected by refrains, it is possible to build one's own progression, the sphere of one's own semiotic relevancy, affects and sharing. On the other hand, the refrain can become a cage, a rigid system for interpreting references and existential paths that are compulsively repetitive.

Schizoanalysis intervenes precisely at these points of the refrain's neurotic hardening. Here analysis is no longer understood as the interpretation of symptoms and the search for a latent meaning pre-existing the neurotic fixation. Analysis is the creation of new centers of attention capable of producing a bifurcation, a deviation from the track, a rupture within the closed circuit of obsessive repetition able to inaugurate a new horizon of possibilities for vision and experience.

*Chaosmosis* is situated within a specific historical dimension, that of the mists and miasmas that began to spread at the beginning of the 1990s and that today, fifteen years later, seem to have invaded every space of the atmosphere, infosphere and psychosphere.

Breathing has become difficult, almost impossible: as a matter of fact, one suffocates. One suffocates every day and the symptoms of suffocation are disseminated all along the paths of daily life and the highways of planetary politics.

Our chances for survival are few: we know it. There are no more maps we can trust, no more destinations for us to reach. Ever since its mutation into semiocapitalism, capitalism has swallowed the exchange-value machine not only for the different forms of life, but also of thought, imagination, and hope. There is no alternative to capitalism.

Should we then place old age at the center of our discourse, like Deleuze and Guattari did in their introduction to *What is Philosophy?* Old age is no longer a marginal and rare phenomenon, like it was in the past when old people were considered to bring precious knowledge to the community. Senility is becoming the condition for the majority of a humanity deprived of the courage to bet on the future, since the future has become an obscure and scary dimension.

Today old age is becoming the average social condition of the majority, while at the same time it also becomes the condition that best expresses the metaphor of the energy loss affecting the human race. Libidinal energy declines once the world becomes too fast to be elaborated according to the slow timing of emotions and once entropy dominates cerebral cells. The decline of libidinal energy and entropy are two processes whose sense is in fact the same. The social brain is decomposing as it does in Jonathan Franzen's *The Corrections*. Alzheimer's is becoming a metaphor for a future in which it is difficult to remember the reason for things while the new video-electronic generations seem to be dragged by vortexes of panic until they fall into the spiral of depression. The question of sensibility becomes one with politics: and not even the redefinition of an ethical perspective can set it aside. At the beginning of the new millennium, the end of modernity is announcing itself as the end of our humanist heritage. Hyper-capitalism is emancipating itself from its Western heritage and its so-called "values," but this unveils a terrible sight: without the heritage of Humanism and the Enlightenment, capitalism is a regime of pure, endless and inhuman violence.

The mind is put to work in conditions of economic and existential precariousness. Living time is subjected to work through a fractal dispersion of both consciousness and experience, reducing the coherence of lived time to fragments. The psychosphere has become the scene of a nightmare, and the relation between human beings is deprived of its humanistic surface. The body of the other is no longer within the reach of an empathic perception: slavery, torture, and genocide become normal procedures for elaborating otherness in a-sympathetic conditions. The violent logic of belonging replaces the universality of modern rationality. For the brains decomposing in the big Infosphere mixer, God seems to be the natural path to salvation, while of course it is instead the usual infernal trick. Religious fundamentalism and the cult of purity now join with ignorance and depression to nourish ethnicism and nationalism.

The world landscape is becoming "Islamized" in various ways: submission becomes the dominant form of relation between individuals and groups. While the collective dimension is deprived of any energy coming from desire and reduced to a skeleton of fear and necessity, adhesion to a group becomes compulsive and mandatory. And conformism is the last refuge for souls left without desire or autonomy.

## Ethics and sensibility

In this narrow passage it is the very notion of ethical consciousness that needs to be rethought. Ethical consciousness cannot be founded on the binomial of Reason and Will—as during the modern period. The roots of rationalism have been forever erased, and rationalism cannot be the major direction of the planetary humanism we must conceive.

Today the ethical question is posed as a question of the soul, that is to say of the sensibility animating the body, making it capable of opening sympathetically towards the other. The chemical and linguistic soul we are talking about is the field where a recomposition of bodies can happen.

A new conceptualization of humanism must be founded on an aesthetic paradigm, since it has to take root in sensibility. The collapse of modern ethics needs to be interpreted as a generalized cognitive disturbance, as the paralysis of empathy in the social psychosphere. The acceleration of the mediasphere, the separation of consciousness from the corporeal experience, the de-eroticization of public spaces in the digital realm and the diffusion of competitive principles in every fragment of social life: these are the causes of the dis-empathy diffused in social action, of the diffused cyclothymia, and the alternate waves of panic and depression in the psychosphere. The aesthetic paradigm needs to be considered as the foundation of psychoanalysis, as an ecological therapy for the mind.

Guattari and Deleuze did not employ the vaguely apocalyptic tones I am using here, I know, yet I did not swear to be eternally faithful to my two masters. Today, the rhetoric of desire—the most important and creative contribution that the authors of *Anti-Oedipus* brought to the movements of hope—seems exhausted to me, waiting for a dimension and a movement capable of renewing it. In their last two books, and in *Chaosmosis* in particular, the rhetoric of desire seems already attenuated, if not silenced. What emerges instead is the awareness of the entropy of sense in existential experience and historical perspective, the consciousness of fading, aging and death. This is just what we need today: an awareness of depression that would not be depressing.

**Art as chaoid**

Within Semiocapital, then, the production of value tends to coincide with semiotic production. Pressed by economic competition, the production of accelerated and proliferating signs ends up functioning like a pathogenic factor, congesting the collective psyche that is becoming the primary object of exploitation.

Mental alienation is no longer a metaphor, as it was in the industrial epoch: it becomes, rather, a specific diagnosis. Psychopathy is the word we can use to refer to the effects of the economic mobilization of attention. Abstracted from the historicist field of problems once integrating it, the word "alienation" is replaced by words capable of measuring the effects of exploitation on cognitive activity: panic, anxiety, depression. The psychopathological lexicon becomes a way to diagnose the psychic disturbances affecting the social mind everywhere.

Sensibility is directly invested: this is why in *Chaosmosis*, his last book, Guattari places the aesthetic paradigm at the core of his therapeutic and political perspective.

With the word "aesthetic," he refers to two different issues: sensibility and its modeling by imaginary machines, mass mythologies and mediatic projections. He also refers to artistic creation: the production of refrains, perceptive tunings of a peculiar kind, which are constantly on the run, and incessantly renewing themselves. This is why the possible (not exclusive) therapeutic function of signs, movements and words is founded in the aesthetic domain.

In this sphere we can understand illness, the inoculation of psychopathogenic germs on the part of the imaginary machine, but also the perspective of therapeutic action.

Guattari says that art is a chaoid, a temporary organizer of chaos, a fragile architect of shared happiness and a common map of the imaginary.

Art is the process of producing refrains, the creation of tuned rhythms.

With the word "refrain," Guattari refers to rhythmic rituals, temporary and singular projective structures that make harmony (or disharmony) possible. This harmony (this disharmony) molds the field of desire.

Therefore the structures produced and determined by desire are not eternal, and they are not models preexisting the singular imagination: they are temporary realizations of desire, maps that allow those sharing a journey to recognize their direction and meaning. The territory they cross does not preexist any map of desires. Rather, it is the map that secretes the territory: the map of desire produces the roads we travel.

Desire is the creation of centers that attract collective libidinal energy, polarizations of the Unconscious, and magnetisms structuring the surrounding objects according to a certain pattern.

"Art is a chaoid" means precisely this: that art builds devices that can temporarily model chaos.

> "Art transforms chaotic variability into chaoid [...] Art struggles with chaos but it does so in order to render it sensory."[12]

In the last years of his life, once art and therapy fully demonstrated they were the same thing, and militant existence confirmed it, Guattari summarized his positions in these terms:

> "My perspective involves shifting the human and social sciences from scientific paradigms towards ethico-aesthetic paradigms. It's no longer a question of determining whether the Freudian Unconscious or the Lacanian Unconscious provide scientific answers to the problems of the psyche. From now on these models, along with the others, will only be considered in terms of the production of subjectivity— inseparable as much from the technical and institutional apparatuses which promote it as from their impact on psychiatry, university teaching or the mass media [...]. Psychoanalytic treatment confronts us with a multiplicity of cartographies."[13]

## Schizoanalysis, therapy, and art

Freudian and Lacanian theories, as any other mythology of the soul, need to be taken for what they are: creations of self-imaginations, projects of exploration in the unconscious which create their own territory while narrating it. This is what schizoanalysis does instead: it replaces interpretation with a proliferation of escape plans and possible existential patterns; creative proliferation replaces interpretative reductions.

The process of the cure cannot be understood (by familial psychoanalysis, or normalizing psychoanalysis) as the reduction of deviant psyches to socially recognized linguistic and psychological behavioral norms. On the contrary, it will have to be understood as the creation of psychological cores capable of transforming a certain mental cartography into a livable space, a happy singularization of the self. This is the task of schizoanalysis: to follow the delirium in order to make it coherent and accessible to friendship both with the self and the other; to dissolve the identity-fixed clots that harden the refrain; to link refrains and to reopen the channels of communication between individual drifts and the cosmic game.

Therapy needs to be understood as a chaoid similar to art.

> "Analysis is no longer the transferential interpretation of symptoms as a function of preexisting, latent content, but the invention of a new catalytic nucleus capable of bifurcating existence. A singularity, a rupture of sense, a cut, a fragmentation, the detachment of a semiotic content—in a Dadaist or surrealist manner—can originate mutant nuclei of subjectivation."[14]

Therefore the therapeutic question can be described as the dissolution of the mind's obsessive clotting, the formation of desiring centers capable of determining a deterriorialization of action, of shifting the mental focus and determining the conditions for a collective subjectivation.

The passive estrangement named alienation, the painful estrangement from the self, must then be overturned to become a delirious, creative, refocusing estrangement.

For Guattari, psychological pain can be tied to issues of obsessive focalization.

The infinite desiring energy is discharged through compulsive repetition and exhausts itself in this repetitive investment. The therapeutic method adopted by schizoanalysis is that of a new focalization and shift of attention. The creativity of the therapeutic act consists in the capacity of finding a way to escape: a schizo virus capable of producing a deviation from the obsessive one.

Once again therapy reveals its affinities with artistic creation.

If desire is not dependent on structures, even less does it have to be considered a natural phenomenon, an authentic or instinctual manifestation. There is a naïve reading of Guattari's and Deleuze's theories, according to which desire would be a primal propulsive force to which we need to return in order to find the energy for rebellion and autonomy. This is a simplifying and misleading reading.

Desire is not at all natural. Social desire (modeling, invading and recomposing the structures of collective life) is culturally formed. It is the semiotic environment that models desire, the cloud of signs surrounding the bodies, connoting spaces and projecting ghosts. If we think of the function that advertising has in the production of contemporary desire, we easily realize how desire is nothing else but a contaminating field of battle.

Political communication also works essentially on flows of desire, redirecting collective investments of desiring energy: the astonishing overturning of the political front that took place beginning in the 1980s and the sweeping victory of the capitalist offensive after years of social autonomy and workers' struggles can be explained only as the consequence of an extraordinary transformation in the collective investment of desire.

Privatization, competition, individualism—aren't these the consequences of a catastrophic overturning of the investments of collective desire? The loss of solidarity deprived workers of any political force and created the conditions for the hyper-exploitation of precarious labor, reducing the labor force to a condition of immaterial slavery: couldn't this be the effect of a fantastic disruption and perversion of collective desire?

After a long period of absolute domination by semiocapital, that is to say of economic principles modeling the collective imagination, nuclei of acquisitional and competitive obsession were formed within the social Unconscious. The refrains circulating in the social unconscious became rigid, congested, aggressive and terrified.

Political action needs to be conceived first of all as a shift in the social investments of desire. The obsessive nuclei stratified in the social imagination produce pathologies: panic, depression and attention deficit disorders. These clots need to be dissolved, avoided, deterritorialized.

There is no possibility of political resistance to the absolute domination of Semiocapitalism, since its foundations are not exterior, residing neither in the military violence of the state, nor in the economic corporate abuse: they are incorporated in the pathogenic refrains that pervasively entered the collective unconscious.

Political action must happen therefore according to modalities analogous to therapeutic intervention. Political action and therapy both need to start from the obsessive loci of desire. Their task is to refocus our attention on deterritorializing points of attraction, so that new investments of desire become possible, which will be autonomous from competition, acquisition, possession, and accumulation.

**Debt, time, wealth**

The postmodern domination of capitalism is founded on the refrain of wealth, understood as cumulative possession. A specific idea of wealth took control of the collective mind which values accumulation and the constant postponing of pleasurable enjoyment. But this idea of wealth (specific to the sad science of economics) transforms life into lack, need and dependence. To this idea of wealth we need to oppose another idea: wealth as time—time to enjoy, travel, learn and make love.

Economic submission, producing need and lack, makes our time dependent, transforming our life into a meaningless run towards nothingness. Indebtedness is the basis for this refrain.

In 2006, the book *Generation Debt* (subtitled: *Why now is a terrible time to be young*) was published in the United States. The author, Anya Kamenetz considers a question that finally came to the forefront of our collective attention in 2007, but has been fundamental to capitalism for a long time: debt.

Anya Kamenetz's analysis refers especially to young people taking out loans in order to study. For them, debt functions like a symbolic chain whose effects are more powerful than the real metal chains formerly used in slavery.

This new model of subjugation goes through a cycle of capture, illusion, psychological submission, financial trap and finally, pure and simple obligation to work.

Imagine a middle class teenager in the United States, willing to plan a university education, in order to acquire the professional competence that will allow him access to the job market. This poor fellow, who believed in the fairy tales of Neo-liberalism, really believes that he has the chance for achieving a guaranteed happy life thanks to serious work and study.

But how can s/he pay a tuition of thousands of dollars a year, plus the expenses for room and board in a distant city? If you were not raised in a family of high finance thieves, the only way is to ask for a loan from a bank. Like Faust on his way home one night, who meets a little dog that followed him to his room and finally reveals itself to be Mephistopheles, so our young fellow meets a financial operator working for a bank that accords him/her a loan. Once you sign, your soul belongs to me, says Mephistopheles, forever. Our young fellow signs the loan, goes to university and graduates: after that, his/her life belongs to the bank. S/he will have to start working immediately after graduation, in order to pay back a never ending amount of money, especially when the loan is made at a variable rate of interest, constantly growing with the passage of time. S/he will have to accept any condition of work, any exploitation, any humiliation, in order to pay the loan which follows her wherever s/he goes.

Debt is the creation of obsessive refrains that are imposed on the collective mind. Refrains impose psychological misery thanks to the ghost of wealth, destroying time in order to transform it into economic value. The aesthetic therapy we need—an aesthetic therapy that will be the politics of the times to come—

consists in the creation of dissipating refrains capable of giving light to another modality of wealth, understood as time for pleasure and enjoyment.

The crisis that began in the summer of 2007 has opened a new scene: the very idea of social relation as "debt" is now crumbling apart.

The anti-capitalistic movement of the future won't be a movement of the poor, but of the wealthy. The real wealthy of the future will be those who will succeed in creating forms of autonomous consumption, mental models of need reduction, habitat models for the sharing of indispensable resources. This requires the creation of dissipative wealth refrains, or of frugal and ascetic wealth.

In the virtualized model of semiocapitalism, debt worked as a general frame of investment, but it also became a cage for desire, transforming desire into lack, need and dependency that is carried for life.

Finding a way out of such a dependency is a political task whose realization is not a task for politicians. It's a task for art, modulating and orienting desire, and mixing libidinal flows. It is also a task for therapy, understood as a new focalization of attention, and a shifting of the investments of desiring energy.

**Desire and simulation: Wenders in Tokyo**

In 1983 Wim Wenders went to Tokyo with the idea of making a documentary in homage of Yasujiro Ozu, the great director who had died in 1962.

Using his camera as a notebook, he marked his impressions, meditations and emotions, narrating in black and white, like in an old-fashioned journal, his discovery of a hyper-modern Japan.

The title of his movie is *Tokyo-ga* and it is considered one of Wenders' minor movies. It is not. It is instead from every point of view an extremely important movie. From the perspective of the German director's personal evolution, *Tokyo-ga* marks the passage from the dreamy, slow and nostalgic narration that characterized his 1970s production—*Alice in the Cities*, *Kings of the Road* (*In the Course of Time*)—to his conflicted but fascinated use of electronic technologies, like in his discombobulated but genial film *Until the End of the World*.

His relation with Ozu's cinema is the filter through which Wenders tries to get the sense of the ongoing mutation leading Japanese society (but in fact global society) beyond humanistic and industrial modernity, towards a dimension that cannot yet be named, but appears already as post-humanistic and perhaps even post-human.

Yasujiro Ozu used technology as a support, a prolongation and a possibility for the human gaze and sensory experience, as a power directed towards emotional and conceptual projection. His camera was positioned in such a way that it exalted the centrality of human dimensions: all this happened in pre-war Japan, where the continuity with tradition had not yet been interrupted.

In the sphere of the indefinable hyper-modernity that Wenders records as if he was sketching a map, we are witness to the overturning of the relationship between human intellect and technology, between the human gaze and its electronic prosthesis. Human intellect is becoming little by little (or suddenly) part of the interconnected global Mind, and the human eye an internal function of the video-reticular *panopticon*. From a philosophical point of view *Tokyo-ga* is an extraordinarily lucid summary, extremely aware of the dissolution of the real caused by simulation techniques. Simulation became the central word used in the post-literate lexicon, beginning with the 1980s, when microelectronic technologies spread in every communicative domain and in the production of worlds.

Simulation produces emptiness, a real hole, the disappearance of sensible tangibility, which is replaced by sensible virtuality. All this is already present in Wenders' *Tokyo-ga* (1983).

Wenders describes Japan as the society where an artificial mutation has occurred: life is nothing but a simulation effect. Objects and foods are simulated, social relations themselves are simulated. Wenders takes us with him to a factory of artificial food, where pears and apples, meats and tropical fruits are perfectly reproduced using synthetic materials, in order to simulate real food to be placed in metropolitan restaurants' windows. The director's astonishment at this banal reproduction gives to the movie a pathetic tone, vaguely provincial and nostalgic: the disappearance of food, replaced by wax or plastic, generates nostalgic memories of a world where food was authentic, and we can perceive that, beginning with these apparently minuscule signals, the world has started to disappear.

On the ramparts of a huge stadium, lonely white-clad players hit a little white golf ball with their golf sticks: it makes a long parabola in the air until it finally reaches the ground, mingling with thousands of others. An infinite expanse of isolated individuals unaware of each other's presence, and an infinite number of white golf balls. Then, Wenders takes us inside the long and narrow locales where *pachinko* is played by men of all ages, silent in front of their machine. Without ever talking or looking at each other, they all concentrate on pulling a lever that will send little metal balls moving behind a sheet of glass.

In *Empire of Signs*, a book devoted to his impressions of a trip to Japan, Roland Barthes had described *pachinko* with these words:

"Pachinko is a slot machine. At the counter you buy a little stock of what look like ball bearings; then, in front of the machine (a kind of vertical panel), with one hand you stuff each ball into a hole, while with the other, by turning a flipper, you propel the ball through a series of baffles; if your initial dispatch is just right [...] the propelled ball releases a rain of more balls, which fall into your hand, and you have only to start over again—unless you choose to exchange your winnings for an absurd reward [...].

The pachinko is a collective and solitary game. The machines are set up in long rows; each player standing in front of his panel plays for himself, without looking at his neighbor, whom he nonetheless brushes with his elbow. You hear only the balls whirring through their channels [...]; the parlor is a hive or a factory—the players seem to be working on an assembly line."[15]

Wenders relates the massive diffusion of *pachincko* to the necessity of reducing the psychological pressure caused by the post-war period, liberating the collective mind from the haunting of a terrifying past that had to be forgotten, erased, and removed. At the same time, as Roland Barthes writes, *pachincko* reveals a society where people are perfectly individualized, isolated, lonely, reduced to empty containers of productive time, deprived of their memory and of any form of heroism except for the silent one of productivity.

It is from within film history that Wenders tries to outline the cartography of this mutational phase, and the hyper-modern (and post-human) passage in store for the human race, involved in an evolution that human beings are also observing, spectators and actors at once, but finally spectators more than anything else.

Then the director interviews two people that in the past were collaborators of the great Ozu.

Atsuta, the camera operator who had always worked with the director, shows in various touching sequences the filming techniques elaborated during decades of collaboration. He then reveals that, since Ozu's death twenty years earlier, he had not worked with anyone else: he had not betrayed or switched to other techniques, other forms of sensibility.

Chishu Ryu, who played in all Ozu's films, on the contrary, kept on working. He must sadly admit though, that people stop him on the street, asking for his autograph, certainly not because he had played in *Tokyo Monogatari* (*Tokyo Story*), but because he plays now in the commercials for a brand of biscuits or toothpaste.

With Chishu Ryu, Wenders then visits Yasujiro Ozu's grave. While the camera films the black monolith under which the director rests in peace, Wenders pronounces these words, which seem to me could best introduce a meditation on the present post-humanistic, semiocapitalist hyper-modernity:

"Mu, The Void, it's He who reigns now."

This is not the void that Zen Buddhism talks about, or at least not only that. Wenders says: "now."

The void reigns now. Wenders wants to talk of present actuality, in his nostalgic (heavenly nostalgic) film on Yasujiro Ozu.

We're entering the civilization of emptiness: this is in my reading of Wenders' visit to Tokyo: the city that used to be Ozu's and now belongs to the Demiurge of simulation.

*Tokyo-ga* was produced in 1983. The deep effects of the neoliberal economic turn on social culture were becoming evident: like those of the revolution Nixon had provoked twelve years earlier when he decided to de-link the dollar from gold, abandoning the system of fixed exchange. The financial world fell into indeterminacy, while neo-liberalism, imposing the hegemony of the financial cycle over both economic and social relations, brought to every domain of existence the awareness of the indeterminate, aleatory nature of reality.

The relation between sign and referent disappears: in economic terms, the relation between financial sign and material referent (real production, gold as the measure of financial evaluation) vanishes.

**Desire and simulation: Baudrillard in America**

Microelectronic technologies make the miniaturization of circuits possible and start the microelectronic revolution, whose effects we have seen fully developed in the 1990s. Telematics, the new science integrating mobile phones and informatics, the revolutionary technique to which Simon Nora and Alain Minc devoted a very important book already in 1978, entitled *The Computerization of Society*, prepares for the explosion of the network.

In 1983, Jean Baudrillard wrote a text titled *The Ecstasy of Communication*, for the volume *The Anti-Aesthetic: Essays in Post-Modernism*, edited by Hal Foster and published by Bay Press.

> "There is no longer any system of objects. My first book contains a critique of the object as obvious fact, substance, reality, use-value. There the object was taken as sign, but as sign still heavy with meaning."[16]

In the old world the sign was understood as a bearer of meaning, and the relation between sign and meaning was guaranteed by the external and objective existence of a referent. But this referential logic is abandoned once we enter the domain of generalized indeterminacy. What guarantees the dollar's value once the reference to gold is erased? What guarantees the value of a commodity, once the time of necessary social labor can't be measured anymore? Immaterial technologies transform the time of labor necessary to produce goods into an aleatory time. And what guarantees the meaning of a sign once all signs transgress their codes, once the phantasmagoria of the code becomes the code of phantasmagoria? Only force guarantees the meaning of the monetary sign, as is demonstrated by the despotic exercise of American hegemony. Deregulation does not mean that society is freed from all rules, not at all: it is instead the imposition of monetary rule on all domains of human action. And monetary rules are in fact the sign of a relationship based on power, violence and military abuse.

In those years the scene of reality had been abandoned to enter the scene of simulation. Cinema does not belong to this second order. Cinema belongs to the order of reproduction and expression, not to the order of simulation. In front of the camera there is (or there has been) a real object, a real person: the camera registered that very light, body, those visible materials, reproducing them all on film. In this way conditions were created in order for the director to express himself in a purely Deleuzian and Spinozian sense: to give life to one among the many infinite worlds that language can create.

We enter the domain of simulacra when we move from analogue film to the creation of synthetic images. The synthetic image can indeed be defined as a simulacrum, since it does not presuppose any real object, any material light or prototype, but only the interior lighting of the digital (im)materiality. Simulation is the elimination of the referent which initiates a series of infinite semiotic replications without any foundation.

> "Simulation is precisely this irresistible unfolding, this sequencing of things as though they had a meaning, when they are governed only by artificial *montage* and non-meaning."[17]

Digital replication develops language's power of simulation to its fullest. Digital technology makes possible a process of infinite replication of the sign. The sign becomes a virus eating the reality of its referent. Rapidly, this process of de-signifying replication of the sign produces the effect that Baudrillard calls the desert of the real.

> "America is a giant hologram, in the sense that information concerning the whole is contained in each of its elements. Take the tiniest little place in the desert, any old street in a Mid-West town, a parking lot, a Californian house, a Burger King or a Studebaker, and you have the whole of the US—South, North, East, or West."[18]

The concept of simulation introduces a new perspective within philosophical discourse, a perspective that can be defined as disappearance. Once subtracted from the domain of alphabetic sequentiality and projected into the domain of video-electronic replication, the sign proliferates endlessly, creating a second reality, a synthetic domain that ends up swallowing the first world, the body, and nature.

America, as Baudrillard sees it, is very different from the one seen by Deleuze and Guattari. It is the land of extinction, where the made up and embalmed corpse of reality replaces life, and not the country provided with infinite energy, producing schizoid signs, endlessly reactivated.

Welcome to the desert of the real.

The way Baudrillard refers to schizophrenia is also very different from the way Felix Guattari's schizoanalysis describes it in his exaltation of creativity. Baudrillard does not associate schizophrenia with creative proliferation, but with terror.

I am not saying this to establish who's right, the tiny desiring crowd that declares the creative schizoid power or the lonely spellbound traveler making photographs in the silent desert of a no longer existing real.

The point is not who's right or wrong. But it is necessary to retrace the processes occurring at the end of the last century using concepts that not only can describe, but also transform them: I don't mean transform the world, but to transform the relation between singularities and world projections.

**The Baudrillard-Foucault debate**

In the mid-1970s, the philosophical scene is cleared of its Hegelian heritage. The concept of alienation is abandoned, since alienation in social practice has been turned into estrangement. The repetitiveness of the productive routine has been turned into the refusal to work and sabotage, the loneliness of the individual at the assembly line has been transformed into subversive community and collective organization. In the 1970s the bodies revolted forgetting their souls: bodies reclaimed their own spaces.

"The soul is the jail of the body," read a feminist sign on the streets of Bologna in 1977, a time when all thoughts and expectations were written, screamed and exposed.

In those years the question of subjectivity appears under a new light: there is no longer any Subject (*upokeimenos*) charged with realizing the truth of history, but there are individuals meeting with other singularities. The historical (or narrative) agent is liberated from the structure, has no more blueprints to follow, no script to play.

In France, during the mid 1970s, a philosophical debate developed, investing issues left open and undefined by the collapse of the dialectic structure and in particular the question of the formation of both the subject and power.

This debate placed Jean Baudrillard on one side, and Michel Foucault and the authors of *Anti-Oedipus* on the other. That debate marked a decisive philosophical passage.

On the side of Deleuze, Guattari and Foucault, and also of their pupils (among whom I humbly include myself), there has always been a certain resistance to discuss the controversy with Baudrillard, as if it had been one of those Parisian intellectual scuffles that it is better to avoid.

Now, thirty years later, I believe that it would be important to understand the meaning of that debate, since today we might find in it elements that could be used for finding a new synthesis. What was the object of the controversy?

After publishing his most important book, *Symbolic Exchange and Death* in 1977, Baudrillard published that same year a booklet titled *Forget Foucault*. It is an attack on the theory of power built by Foucault, but Baudrillard's real purpose was to critique the notion of desire itself, and the molecular theory of Deleuze and Guattari.

*Forget Foucault* begins with an interpretation of *Discipline and Punish*. Baudrillard disagrees with Foucault's fundamental thesis in that book, and with his entire analysis of the genealogy of modern power as repressive disciplining of corporeality.

> "One could say a lot about the central thesis of the book: there has never been a repression of sex but on the contrary an injunction against talking about it or voicing it and a compulsion to confess, to express, and to *produce* sex. Repression is only a trap and an alibi to hide assigning an entire culture to the sexual imperative."[19]

Baudrillard's remarks were not directly rebuffed by Foucault, but my thesis is that in some direct or indirect, explicit or implicit way, Foucault later developed his theory taking these into account. Perhaps Baudrillard's objections understood something true, but misunderstood the essential lesson of the "desiring" theories. Baudrillard attacked Foucault's vision of the genealogy of power in order to propose a critique of all the theories that in those years developed a social discourse from libidinal economy and desiring expressivity. Thus he writes:

> "One can only be struck by the coincidence between this new version of power and the new version of desire proposed by Deleuze and Lyotard: but there, instead of a lack or interdiction, one finds the deployment and the positive dissemination of flows and intensities [...]. Micro-desire (that of power) and micro-politics (that of desire) literally merge at the libido's mechanical confines: all that one has to do is miniaturize."[20]

Is there any equivocation in Baudrillard's critique of desiring theory? Yes, there might be: Baudrillard's vision still refers to desire as power, while we have seen that desire needs to be understood as a field.

Yet this equivocation has its reasons, since this equivocation is in fact inscribed in Deleuze's and Guattari's work, and also in

Lyotard's and Foucault's: most of all, this ambiguity is present in the mass culture that in those years dominated the desiring discourse in order to develop a practical critique of late-modern, late-industrial power structures.

But today we are at the end of that form of power, now we have entered a new era and a new dimension. Capitalism is becoming schizo, the acceleration that desire had imposed on social expressivity has been incorporated by the capitalistic machine when it became a post-mechanic, digital machine.

The shift from mechanical to digital, from reproducible to simulative is the shift from the limited to the viral dimension of power.

*Anti-Oedipus* preached acceleration as an escape from capital's time. "*Cours camarade, le vieux monde est derrière toi*"[21]—we screamed in 1968. That was true as long as capital's velocity was the mechanical one of the assembly lines, railways and the printing press. But when microelectronic technologies equip capital with absolute velocity in the real time of simulation, then acceleration becomes the domain of hyper-exploitation.

This is not, let's state it clearly, a merely metaphoric discourse.

Think about workers' struggles. As long as they happened in the industrial factory, the acceleration in workers communication and action placed the owner in a defensive position and was able to defeat structures of control. Slogans circulated rapidly among workers in their factories and neighborhoods, allowing these struggles to become generalized.

Microelectronic technologies have completely reversed this situation: capital conquers the capacity for rapid deterritorialization, transferring production all over the globe, while the timing of workers' organizations remains localized and slow as compared to the one of capitalist globalization.

Baudrillard anticipates this trend with his intuition of an absolute velocity knocking down every form of social communication. On this intuition Baudrillard develops his theory, proclaimed in *Forget Foucault* (and elsewhere), but he never received any explicit reply. Political intentions and discursive effects are different: Baudrillard's intention was denounced by the desiring theory as dissuasive, since his vision destroys the possibility of expecting new processes of subjectivation. Baudrillard, on his part, denounced the desiring vision as an ideological function of the new, reticular, capitalist mode of production.

> "This compulsion towards liquidity, flow, and an accelerated situation of what is psychic, sexual, or pertaining to the body is the exact replica of the force which rules market value: capital must circulate; gravity and any fixed point must disappear; the chain of investments and reinvestments must never stop; value must radiate endlessly and in every direction. This is the form itself which the current realization of value takes. It is the form of capital, and sexuality as a catchword and a *model* is the way it appears at the level of bodies."[22]

Baudrillard's critique is not generous: the description of the mutation in the forms of power and subjectivity is presented as a wish, yet there is something true in his words. Within desiring theory, and the vast movement of thought that Deleuze's, Guattari's and Foucault's books have produced, there is a rhetorical danger if it is not understood that desire is a field and not a force.

This is evident, for instance, in the empty use of the term "multitude" by Negri and Hardt and many others in the last 10 years. They speak of the multitude as if it was a boundless positive energy, a force of liberty that cannot submit to domination in any way. But in 1978, in a booklet entitled *In the Shadow of the Silent Majorities*, Baudrillard already demolished the subversive political use of the concept of multitude, showing its other side, that of the constitutive passivity of the masses.

> "It has always been thought—this is the very ideology of the mass media—that it is the media which envelop the masses. The secret of manipulation has been sought in a frantic semiology of the mass media. But it has been overlooked, in this naïve logic of communication, that *the masses are a stronger medium than all the media*, that it is the former who envelop and absorb the latter—or at least there is no priority of one over the other. The mass and the media are one single process. Mass(age) is the message."[23]

Within the autonomous movement that had been reading passionately Deleuze's and Guattari's books since the 1970s, Baudrillard's position was considered politically dissuasive: it seemed to describe a situation without escapes, hopes for rebellion or possible ruptures. Yet this wasn't true, and is still not true. Baudrillard did acknowledge the dissuasive functioning of a civilization where events are simulated and erased by simulation itself.

> "Deterrence is a very peculiar form of action: it is *what causes something not to take place*. It dominates the whole of our contemporary period, which tends not so much to produce events as to cause something not to occur, while looking as though it is a historical event."[24]

Moreover his theory revealed at this point an extreme resource, that of catastrophe, or rather the resource of a catastrophic implosion.

> "The masses [...] haven't waited for future revolutions nor theories which claim to 'liberate' them by a 'dialectical' movement. They know that there is no liberation, and that a system is abolished only by pushing it into hyperlogic, by forcing it into an excessive practice which is equivalent to a brutal amortization. You want us to consume—O.K., let's consume always more, and anything whatsoever; for any useless and absurd purpose."[25]

Far from sharing the cynicism spread throughout culture in the 1980s and 1990s (the cynicism pervading the French *nouvelle philosophie*—the New Philosophy—as well as the conformist neoliberalism which followed the disillusion of the 1968 generation all over Europe), Baudrillard proposes the strategy of catastrophe. Today, thirty years later, it seems to me that he was not wrong at all.

To the notion of desire Baudrillard opposes that disappearance, or rather the chain Simulation-Disappearance-Implosion.

Simulation is the creation of ghosts without a prototype. An algorithm produces endless chains of information. The effect of semiotic inflation activates the progressive colonization of increasingly larger portions of reality by the informational emulsion. Reality disappears like the Amazonian forest, or a territory devoured by the desert, until the entire context that used to guarantee the living continuity of the community ends up being eliminated by this effect of de-realization and the organism implodes.

## Simulation and libido

Simulation is therefore a projection of signs that neither reproduce nor record any facts, but the effect of the projection of ghosts never preceded by a body. Synthetic morphogenesis is the clearest example of this simulation phenomenon. The image produced by a calculator is the development of an algorithm, not the reproduction of a preexisting reality.

The replication of synthetic images has a viral and boundless character, since the creation of a new simulacrum does not request any investment of energy or matter. Lived experience is thus invaded by the pervasive proliferation of simulacra. Here we can see the origin of a pathology of desire, a sort of cancer reaching the very heart of the libidinal experience. Libidinal energy is attacked by a replicant of a parasitic type, as shown by the phenomenon of synthetic media pornography. "Libidinal parasites" is the formulation used by Matteo Pasquinelli to define this disease in his book *Animal Spirits* (NAI Publishers, 2009).

*Anti-Oedipus* postulated the idea that there is never too much Unconscious, since the Unconscious is not a theatre, but a laboratory: not representation, but expression, to use the language of Spinozian Deleuze.

In his *Expressionism in Philosophy: Spinoza*, Deleuze asserts in fact that:

> "Expression is inherent in substance, insofar as substance is absolutely infinite [...]. Thus infinity has a nature. Merleau-Ponty has well brought out what seems to us now the most difficult thing to understand in the philosophies of the seventeenth century: the idea of a positive infinity as the 'secret of

grand Rationalism'—'an innocent way of setting out in one's thinking from infinity,' which finds its most perfect embodiment in Spinozism."[26]

And also:

"God's absolute essence is the absolutely infinite power of existing and acting; but we only assert this primary power as identical to the essence of God/conditionally upon/an infinity of formally or really distinct attributes. The power of existing and acting is thus absolute formal essence."

And there is more:

"God understands and expresses himself objectively."[27]

Yet all this talking about the infinite power of God tells us nothing about human expressive power, which is not infinite, or about the psychological and physical energy that the human organism has at its disposal, which is not infinite either.

The limited character of libidinal energy brings us back to the theme of depression as collective phenomenon. The semiotic acceleration and the proliferation of simulacra within the mediatized experience of society produce an effect of exhaustion in the collective libidinal energy, opening the way to a panic-depressive cycle. In his text on libidinal parasites, Pasquinelli raises the problem of the thermodynamics of desire, formulating two different hypotheses. One, inspired by the first law of thermodynamics, is the idea that within libidinal exchange there is no loss, but a constant quantity of energy. The other is based on the second law of thermodynamics, and presupposes instead that in any exchange there is a loss: this produces entropy, a loss of order and a dispersion of energy.

Baudrillard sees simulation as the infinite replication of a virus that absorbs desiring energy to the point of exhaustion. A sort of semiotic inflation explodes in the circuits of our collective sensibility, producing effects of mutation that run a pathological course: too many signs, too fast, and too chaotic. The sensible body is subjected to an acceleration that destroys every possibility of conscious decodification and sensible perception.

This is the objection that Baudrillard addresses to the *Anti-Oedipus*.

But isn't this what Deleuze and Guattari are ultimately saying in their last work? In their book on old age, written while they were aging themselves, they ask what philosophy is about, and they answer that philosophy is friendship, and (to use Buddhist language) the Great Compassion: it is the capacity to walk together along the abyss of meaning gaping under our feet. In that last book the two schizo philosophers talk about old age and schizo pain, and the too quick quickening of signs and ideas running away without ever getting caught.

> "We require just a little order to protect us from chaos. Nothing is more distressing than a thought that escapes itself, than ideas that fly off, that disappear hardly formed, already eroded by forgetfulness."[28]

After *Forget Foucault* and the other texts of the mid 1970s, where Baudrillard critiqued the theories of desire and Foucault's genealogy of power, were published, nobody responded to his objections, which seemed provocative or maybe dissuasive. Yet Baudrillard's discourse still produced some effects, and I believe that in their last book Deleuze and Guattari developed their thoughts at a level that implicitly involved the meditation that Baudrillard had proposed. I am not saying that they replied without naming him, and not even that they were thinking of Baudrillard when they wrote their last book. I am simply saying that Baudrillard's critique goes in the same direction of the shifting tones and positions that we can experience reading *What is Philosophy?* after *Anti-Oedipus*. It is not enough to say that *Anti-Oedipus* is a book of youth while, twenty years later *What is Philosophy?* is a book of old age. It is not enough either to say that one is a book of 1968 enthusiasm, and the other a book of the years when the barbarians had won again. It is necessary to consider the conceptual shift that took place in this passage much more deeply.

The entropy of libido that Pasquinelli discusses seems to emerge in Deleuze and Guattari's last book once, having abandoned a certain Spinozian triumphalism, we can admit that libidinal energy is a limited resource.

### The disappearance (and the return) of the event

In the mid-1970s, in the context of the radical culture, we see two opposite models of imagination at work. The schizo vision thinks that the proliferation of desire can endlessly erode all structures of control. The implosive vision sees proliferation as the diffusion of a de-realizing virus. Desire is only the effect of a seduction whose subject is actually a hostage, a victim.

> "The 'molecular revolution' only represents the final stage of 'liberation of energy' (or of proliferation of segments, etc.) up

to the infinitesimal boundaries of the field of expansion which has been that of our culture. The infinitesimal attempt of desire succeeding the infinite attempt of capital. The molecular solution succeeding the molar investment of spaces and the social. The final sparks of the explosive system, the final attempt to still control an energy of confines, or to shrink the confines of energy [...] so as to save the principle of expansion and of liberation."[29]

Subjectivity implodes and in its stead we find only the terror of a catastrophe, or the catastrophe of terror. The proliferation of simulation viruses has swallowed the event. The infinite capacity of replication of the recombining simulator device erases the originality of the event. What is left is suicide.

Baudrillard had already been thinking about the issue of suicide in his 1976 book, where symbolic exchange was accompanied by death.

"It is at least possible to find an even match to oppose third-order simulacra? Is there a theory or a practice which is subversive because it is more aleatory than the system itself, an indeterminate subversion which would be to the order of the code what the revolution was to the order of political economy? Can we fight DNA? Certainly not by means of the class struggle. Perhaps simulacra of a higher logical (or illogical) order could be invented: beyond the current third order, beyond determinacy and indeterminacy. But would they still be simulacra? Perhaps death and death alone, the reversibility of death, belongs to a higher order than the code."[30]

In those years Baudrillard talked about the disappearance of the event, eliminated by the seductive proliferation of simulation. *The Illusion of the End*, a book first published in 1992, is inaugurated by a quote from Elias Canetti:

> "A tormenting thought: as of a certain point, history was no longer *real*. Without noticing it, all mankind suddenly left reality; everything happening since then was supposedly not true."[31]

Baudrillard here writes:

> "One has the impression that events form all on their own and drift unpredictably towards their vanishing point—the peripheral void of the media. Just as physicists now see their particles only as a trajectory on a screen, we no longer have the pulsing of events, but only the cardiogram."[32]

The infinite proliferation of signs occupies the space of attention and imagination up to the point of fully absorbing the libidinal energies of society, depriving the organism of all sensibility towards the pulsations of daily reality. The velocity of semiotic proliferation, unleashed by digital simulation, is so extreme that all circuits of collective sensibility end up being saturated. We could also describe this process in another way. Devices of social control are incorporated in automated systems: political governance are thus replaced by chains of automatisms and incorporated in the productive, communicative, administrative, and technical machinery. The living collectivity has no decisional role any more, on fundamental issues like production and the social distribution of wealth, since the access to the social game requires the adoption of automatic operational systems. At a linguistic level, chains of interpretation are automated in such a way that it's no longer possible to read enunciations that don't respect the preventively inscribed code, that is to say the code of capital accumulation.

In his paradoxical style, and sometimes maybe too quickly, Baudrillard talks about this process, identifying it with the disappearance of the event.

In his *Symbolic Exchange and Death* (1976), using New York skyscrapers as a metaphor for digital simulation, Baudrillard had written (and I read this with a shudder):

"Why has the World Trade Center in New York got *two* towers? All Manhattan's great buildings are always content to confront each other in a *competitive* verticality, from which there results an architectural panorama that is the image of the capitalistic system; a pyramidal jungle, every building on the offensive against every other [...]. This new architecture no longer embodies a competitive system, but a countable one where competition has disappeared in favour of correlation [...]. This architectural graphism belongs to the monopoly: the World Trade Center's two towers are perfect parallelepipeds, four hundred meters high on a square base; they are perfectly balanced and blind communicating vessels. The fact that they are two identical towers *signifies* the end of all competition, the end of every original reference."[33]

But the story does not end here.

After September 11, 2001, in a scandalous text, Baudrillard affirms the return of the event. With the collapse of the two WTC buildings, the spell of simulation also ended together with the infinite duplication effect whose metaphor had already been found in his 1976 text on the Twin Towers, where they had appeared as the towers of digital replication.

*The Spirit of Terrorism* is a text written immediately after the most spectacular terrorist attack in history. The word "spectacular" assumes here a double meaning, a paradoxical character, since here the spectacle is precisely the collapse of all spectacle, and that implosion provokes an explosion. Baudrillard's purpose in this text is to celebrate the return of the event beyond the cages of simulation.

> "With the attacks on the World Trade Center in New York, we might even be said to have before us the absolute event, the 'mother' of all events, the pure event uniting within itself all the events that have never taken place."[34]

The immense concentration of decision-making power put into play by semiocapitalism already lends itself to catastrophic events. That intolerable suicidal action unveiled the vanity of power's infinite strength, confronting it with a form of escape that reduces it to zero, to its ashes.

Death, suicide more precisely, is the unforeseeable event that restores the chain of events. Since that day suicide became visible as the leading actor on the scene of third millennium history. No matter what other perspective we might decide to adopt to look at twentieth-first century history—capitalist dogma, fanaticism or despair—suicide is the truth hidden by official discourses, by both the rhetoric of unlimited growth and the rhetoric of religious or national fundamentalism.

## Suicide

Since the day twelve young Arabs raised hell in Manhattan, immolating themselves in their airliners and launching the first post-modern war, suicide became the leading actor of world history. Suicide is not a new form of radical protest. In 1904, for instance, the Dutch landed in Bali to subject the island to their colonial power. The Hindu population, proud of its own diversity in the archipelago, fiercely opposed the Dutch invasion. After several battles had occurred, the Dutch were ready to attack Denpassar royal palace. All dressed in white, the *raja* and his court moved towards the Dutch until they were very close to their invaders. All men following the king took out their swords and drove them into their chests, enacting a ritual suicide that in Balinese language is called *puputan*. More than nine hundred men fell to the ground under the astonished eyes of the Dutch. The event's effect was traumatic for the Dutch people's consciousness, beginning the process of crisis in the colonial polices of that country.

It was at the end of World War II that Japanese generals decided to use suicide as an arm of destruction and not simply as an ethical protest. To resist the Americans, who by then were prevailing, they ordered young aviation officers to launch themselves against the enemies' navy. The word "kamikaze," meaning "divine wind," became synonymous with suicidal destructive fury. In her book *Kamikaze Diaries: Reflections of Japanese Student Soldiers* (Chicago, University of Chicago Press, 2006), the Japanese researcher Emiko Ohnuki-Tierney proves that the young pilots were not at all enthusiastic about the destiny that had been assigned to them. By publishing their letters, the author shows that in general the kamikazes were not consenting, and that the higher levels of hierarchy (none of whom was immolated) forced them to take off with airplanes that only had enough fuel to reach the objective (an enemy ship), but not to return.

What is the difference between those ordering a suicide and those ordering a regular bombing, between the sheikh sending desperate youths to blow themselves up in the middle of a crowd, and the U.S. general ordering airplane pilots to bomb a civilian neighborhood?

Aggressive suicide, therefore, is not a new phenomenon, yet in today's context it is terribly more disturbing, not only because anybody who is determined and prepared enough could have access to instruments of destruction and extermination, but also because murderous suicide is no longer a rare marginal phenomenon: it has become a spreading manifestation of contemporary despair. At the origin of murderous suicides, as of any other form of self-directed violence, there is no political reason, or a strategic-military intention, but a form of pain that affects not only Islamic youth. The epidemic of unhappiness infecting the world in the epoch of capitalism's triumph has generated a wave of aggressive suicide in every area of the globe.

Advertising reasserts at every street corner, at every moment, day and night, the freedom of infinite consumption, the joys of property and of victory through competition. In the 1990s, capitalism mobilized an immense intellectual, creative, and psychological energy in order to start the valorization process of the collective intellectual network. But by imposing an unlimited systematic exploitation on the human mind, the productive acceleration created the conditions for an extraordinary psychological breakdown. "Prozac culture" was another name for the *emerging new economy*.

Hundreds of thousands of Western economic operators and managers made innumerable decisions under conditions of chemical euphoria, while they were "high" from their abuse of psychotropic drugs. But the human organism cannot take endless chemical euphoria and productive fanaticism: at some point, it begins to surrender. As happens with patients affected by bipolar disorder, euphoria is replaced by a long-term depression hitting the very source of one's own motivations, entrepreneurship, self-esteem, desire and sex appeal. We cannot fully understand the crisis of the new economy without taking into account the fact that it coincided with a Prozac-crash.

The cognitive worker's individual depression is not a consequence of the economic crisis, but its very reason. It would be easy to imagine that depression is a consequence of business going badly: after years happily spent working with profit, stocks' values collapsed and the new brain workers fell into a deep depression.

This is not the case.

Depression comes from the fact that our emotional, physical, and intellectual energy can't bear the rhythm imposed by competition and chemical-ideological euphoria inducers for long. The market is a psycho-semiotic space, where one can find signs and expectations for meaning, desires and projections. There is an energetic crisis that affects mental and psychic energies. Once this crisis exploded, a new effort was made to motivate the depressed Western psychology with a powerful amphetamine therapy: war. But only a sick person would take amphetamines as a reaction to a depressive crisis. The most likely result will be deeper and deeper relapses.

It is not my intention to put the terrorist suicides of Islamic *shahid* and the *bipolar disorder* affecting Western productive minds on the same level. I am simply saying that these are two convergent pathologies, two different manifestations of the unbearable pain affecting both the hyper-stimulated and competitive psychologies of those who see themselves as winners, and the rancorous ones of the humiliated.

By reducing murderous suicide to political categories, we can only grasp its final manifestations, not its source. The unbearable pain stemming from humiliation, despair, loss of hope in the future, and a feeling of inadequacy and loneliness, and not the strategic intentions of *jihad*, produces suicides. These feelings belong not only to Chechnyan women whose husbands and brothers were killed by Russian soldiers, nor do they belong only to Arab youth subjected to Western violence as to an intolerable humiliation. These feelings of loneliness and loss of meaning are spreading in every place where the triumph of capitalism has subjugated time, life and emotions to the hellish rhythms of automated competition.

The mass production of unhappiness is the topic of our times. The talk of the day is the extraordinary success of the Chinese capitalist economy; meanwhile in 2007 the Central Committee of the Communist Party had to deal with wide-spreading suicides in China's countryside.

Until when will we be able to contain this phenomenon? Until when can we avoid that the rage and despair of one billion excluded people will come and spoil the party of the three hundred million integrated ones? Suicidal terrorism is only one chapter in the contemporary epidemic, although the most explosive and sanguinary. It might happen in one's own tiny isolated room, or in the middle of a crowd at a subway station: suicide is not a response to political motivations, but to pain, unhappiness and despair. Ever since capital's triumph started eroding every domain of life and public life was invaded by competition, velocity and aggressiveness, unhappiness has been spreading everywhere like a forest fire, and not only in areas dominated by Islamism. Now suicide is tending to become the first cause of death among youth everywhere. A few days ago newspapers informed the public that there are traces of Prozac in London's tap water: 24 million British citizens consume anti-depressants.

In 2007 the newspaper *China Today* reported that despite the full economic boom, two hundred thousand people commit suicide every year, and the numbers are growing. In Japan there is a word (*karoshi*) referring to the kind of overwork able to push people to commit suicide. East Japan Railways, one among the several Japanese railway companies, has taken the decision to install big mirrors all along Tokyo station platforms. The idea is to make desperate people on the verge of suicide reconsider as they see their reflected image.

That doesn't seem like the best therapy.

Is there any remedy to the wave of psychopathologies that seems to have submerged the world while smiling faces promise safety, comfort, warmth and success from advertising signboards? It may be that social issues can no longer receive answers from politics, and need to be referred to psychotherapy. Perhaps the answer is that it is necessary to slow down, finally giving up economistic fanaticism and collectively rethink the true meaning of the word "wealth." Wealth does not mean a person who owns a lot, but refers to someone who has enough time to enjoy what nature and human collaboration place put within everyone's reach. If the great majority of people could understand this basic notion, if they could be liberated from the competitive illusion that is impoverishing everybody's life, the very foundations of capitalism would start to crumble.

## Pathogenic alterity

In his film *Persona*, Bergman treats the theme of alterity according to existentialist categories: as malaise, but also as a project of estrangement and suspension of the communicative circuits. Elisabeth Vogler is an actress who during a theater performance stops talking completely, as if affected by a sudden illness, or paralysis. Doctors visit her and their medical reports say that she's perfectly healthy both physically and mentally. Yet Elisabeth keeps on living in complete silence. She's taken to a clinic, where Alma, an extremely competent, brilliant and chatty nurse, takes care of her. The two women develop an intense relationship. In order to complete her therapy, the nurse accompanies Elisabeth to a house by the sea. The two women start getting lost in each other, exchanging their masks. Alma speaks a lot, telling of experiences from her sentimental life and past, while Elisabeth listens to her, apparently involved, despite her silence.

In Latin the word *persona* refers to the "mask": Jung suggests considering it the artificial personality adopted by individuals, consciously or unconsciously, even in contrast with their own characters, in order to protect and defend themselves, deceiving the world that surrounds them in order to adapt to it.
Bergman sees the question of alterity through the schizophrenic figure of the split self, or of double personality. Therefore identity is defined through a game of isolation and enclosure. It is the context of a repressive society that pushes for a compulsive definition of individual masks. In the cultural context where Bergman conceives his film, alienation is the metaphor for the relation between body and soul: a repressive disappearance of the soul.

Forty years later, in a totally different context, Kim Ki Duk made a film that proposed the question of alterity as the game of identities' proliferation and expressive excess. *Time* is the title of his work, and it tells the story of changing one's physical mask thanks to the intervention of aesthetic surgery.

Bergman's title *Persona* refers to a meditation on the identifying mask. Kim Ki Duk works instead around the concept of multiplicity and the many masks that we can assume: that is to say the dis-identifying and proliferating mask. In the age of aesthetic surgery, the multiplicity of masks does not only represent the possibility to be at once different agents of enunciation, but refers specifically to the opportunity of assuming different faces, changing the physical aspect, the place and modality of the enunciation.

*Time* begins in front of the door of an Aesthetic Surgery Clinic, of which there are many in South Korea. Kim Ki Duk's film tells us the story of a man and a woman. They make love and she tells him of her fear of being abandoned because he will end up falling in love with another woman—I need to become another, in order for you to fall in love with me: make love to me as if I were somebody else, tell me what you feel and think. Finally, obsessed by this thought, she decides to become another woman. She goes and sees a surgeon, asking him to change her face and features, so that she becomes unrecognizable. The surgeon advises her that her features are so sweet and delicate that she has no reason to undergo surgery. But she insists; apparently in South Korea, sooner or later half of the women request plastic surgery to change their features. Meanwhile, the man is desperate because of the disappearance of his beloved. He looks for her without success and finally thinks she will never come back to him, until he meets another woman; we know she is his lover, who has become another woman. She seduces him, but the young man's heart belongs to the other one, who has disappeared. At this point she tells him the truth and he has a furious reaction. As a revenge, the man goes to the same surgeon who made his girlfriend unrecognizable, and he asks for the same treatment, so that nobody will be able to recognize him anymore.

Deep identity and the exterior physical aspect, body and soul, and most of all the theme of alterity are the conceptual basis for this film. Kim Ki Duk's language is extremely simple and yet very powerful, dramatic and emotionally involving in many scenes, as when the woman goes back to the Aesthetic Surgery Clinic, desperate for having become someone else, wearing the mask that is now her own face, transformed by the surgeon. Desire is the infinite game of alterity: this is the starting point of the drama we've been told here.

"I want to be another since desire is a constant shifting from one object to another."

Yet we can't underestimate the theme of simulation: aesthetic surgery makes possible a shifting of the object, since it is capable of producing forms that are not copies of a prototype, but synthetic images that have become embodied. Desire and simulation here play their last, most desperate game since it takes place in a physical body where the soul has been captured.

The virtually infinite multiplication of the object of desire is the essential character of the pathologies of our times. It is no longer the absence, or repression, or the prohibition of touching the object. The Other proliferates as an unreachable and unlimited object of consumption, as the virtual substitute of a no longer possible erotic alterity. The Other becomes pornography, since it is always subtracted to enjoyment as it becomes the object of an infinite desire that exhausts the limited libidinal energy of real human beings.

## Malaise and depression

Twentieth century antiauthoritarian theories were directly or indirectly influenced by Freud's notion of repression, on which he focused his *Civilization and Its Discontents*.

> "It is impossible to overlook the extent to which civilization is built up upon a renunciation of instinct, how much it presupposes precisely the non-satisfaction (by suppression, repression or some other means?) of powerful instincts. This 'cultural frustration' dominates the large fields of social relationships between human beings. As we already know, it is the cause of the hostility against which all civilizations have to struggle."[35]

According to Freud, repression is an essential and constitutive aspect of social relations. In the mid-twentieth century, between the 1930s and the 1960s, European critical theories analyzed the relation existing between the anthropologic dimension of alienation and the historical dimension of liberation. Sartre's vision, as exposed in his *Critique of Dialectical Reason* (1964), is directly influenced by Freud's theories, and recognizes the anthropologically constitutive, and therefore unavoidable, character of alienation. On the contrary, Marxist theory in its historicist and dialectic variants considers alienation a historically determined phenomenon that can be overcome through the abolition of capitalist social relations.

In his 1929 essay, Freud anticipates this debate, criticizing the naïveté of dialectics:

> "The communists believe that they have found the path to deliverance from our evils. According to them, man is wholly

> good and is well-disposed to his neighbor; but the institution of private property has corrupted his nature [...]. If private property were abolished, all wealth held in common, and everyone allowed to share in the enjoyment of it, ill-will and hostility would disappear among men [...]. I have no concern with any economic criticism of the communist system; I cannot enquire into whether the abolition of private property is expedient or advantageous. But I am able to recognize that the psychological premises on which the system is based are an untenable illusion."[36]

According to Freud modern capitalism, as every civil system, is founded on a necessary repression of individual libido and the sublimating organization of the collective libido. This intuition is then expressed in many different ways in 20th-century thought.

In the context of Freudian psychoanalysis, our "discontent" is constitutive and inevitable, and psychoanalytic theory offers to heal, through language and anamnesis, the neurotic forms that it might provoke. The philosophical culture of existentialist inspiration shares Freud's firm belief that constitutive alienation is unavoidable and that libidinal drives are repressed.

On the contrary, in the context of Marxist and antiauthoritarian theories, repression needs to be considered as a socially determined form that social action can eliminate by liberating productive and desiring energies already belonging to the real movement of society.

In both of these philosophic scenes however, the concept of repression plays a fundamental role, since it explains the neurotic pathologies dealt with by psychoanalytic theory while at the same time elucidating the capitalistic social contradiction, whose abolishment revolutionary movements want to make possible in order to overcome exploitation and alienation itself.

> "It is impossible to overlook the extent to which civilization is built up upon a renunciation of instinct, how much it presupposes precisely the non-satisfaction (by suppression, repression or some other means?) of powerful instincts." [Freud]

In the 1960s and 1970s the concept of repression was left in the background of political discourse. The political influence of desire was emphasized in opposition to repressive mechanisms, but this way of thinking often ended up becoming a conceptual and political trap. As for instance in 1977 Italy: after the wave of arrests following the February and March insurrections, the movement chose to call a September meeting in Bologna on the question of repression. This was a conceptual mistake: choosing repression as our major topic of discussion, we entered the narrative machine of power, losing our capacity of imagining new forms of life, asymmetrical with respect to power and therefore independent from it. Yet at the end of the twentieth century, the entire question of repression seems to vanish and relinquish the social scene. The dominant pathologies of our times are no longer neurotic, determined by a repression of libido, but rather schizo-pathologies, produced by the expressive explosion of the *just do it*.

### Structure and desire

The antiauthoritarian theories of the 1970s emerge from a Freudian conceptual domain even if they expand and overturn its historical horizons. In *Eros and Civilization*, Marcuse proclaims the timeliness of the liberation of collective eros. Repression compresses technology's and knowledge's potentialities by forbidding their full development, but critical subjectivity develops its action precisely by making possible the full expression of society's libidinal and productive potentialities, thus creating the conditions for the full realization of the pleasure principle.

The analysis of modern society is intertwined with the description of disciplinary instruments modeling social institutions and the public discourse in a repressive way. The recent publication of Foucault's 1979 seminars (particularly the seminar devoted to "the birth of biopolitics") has forced us to move the focus of Foucault's theory from repressive discipline to the creation of biopolitical control devices. Yet in his works devoted to the genealogy of modernity (specifically in *Madness and Civilization*, *Birth of the Clinic*, *Discipline and Punish*), in his own way Foucault still moves within the domain of the "repressive" paradigm.

Despite their open abandonment of the Freudian domain with the *Anti-Oedipus*, Deleuze and Guattari also remain within the field of problems delimited by Freud's 1929 essay *Civilization and its discontents*. Desire is the driving force of the movement both across society and individual experiences, yet desiring creativity has to deal constantly with the repressive war machine that capitalistic society places in every corner of existence and the imagination.

The concept of desire cannot be flattened out in a reading of the "repressive" kind. On the contrary, in *Anti-Oedipus* the concept of desire is opposed to that of lack. The field of lack produced dialectical philosophy, on which twentieth century politics built its (mis)-fortunes: it is the field of dependency, and not of autonomy. Lack is a specific product of the economic regime, of religious and psychiatric domination. Processes of erotic and political subjectivation cannot be founded on lack, but on desire as creation.

From this point of view, Deleuze and Guattari let us understand that repression is nothing but a projection of desire. Desire is not the manifestation of a structure but has the creative power to build a thousand structures. Desire can stiffen structures, transforming them into obsessive refrains. Desire sets traps for itself.

Yet in the analytical frameworks deriving from Foucault's genealogy and Deleuze's and Guattari's creationism prevails a vision of subjectivity as force, as the reemergence of repressed desire against the repressive social sublimation: an anti-repressive, or rather an expressive vision.

The relation between structure and desire is the turning point in Guattari's schizoanalytic theory, leading him outside of Lacanian Freudism's influence. Desire cannot be understood through structure, as a possible variant depending on invariable mathematical models. Creative desire produces infinite structures, and among them even those functioning as apparatuses of repression.

But in order to really exit the Freudian framework, we need to wait for Baudrillard, whose theories looked dissuasive to us in those years. Jean Baudrillard draws a different landscape: in his works of the early 1970s (*The System of Objects*, *The Consumer Society*, "Requiem for the Media" and finally *Forget Foucault*) Baudrillard maintains that desire is the driving force of capital's development and that the ideology of liberation corresponds to the full domination of the commodity: the new imaginary dimension is not repression, but simulation, proliferation of simulacra, seduction. Expressive excess is for Baudrillard the essential core of an overdose of reality.

> "The real is growing like the desert [...] Illusion, dreams, passion, madness and drugs, but also artifice and simulacrum—these were reality's natural predators. They have all lost energy, as though struck down by some dark, incurable malady."[37]

Baudrillard foresees the tendency that would become dominant in the next decades: in his analysis, simulation modifies the relation between subject and object, forcing the subject to accept the subaltern position of the seduced. The active party is not the subject, but the object. Consequentially, the entire field of problems related to alienation, repression, and discontent. In his latest years (in the much quoted work on disciplinary societies and society of control) Deleuze does seem to question Foucault's notion of discipline and the different theoretical architectures descending from it: he seems to go in the direction that Baudrillard had followed since the early 1970s. I am not interested in comparing the theory of simulation with the theory of desire, even if one day this comparison will need to be developed. I am interested in the psychopathologic scene emerging in the years of passage from late industrial society to semio-capitalism, that is to say a form of capitalism based on immaterial labor and the explosion of the Infosphere.

Overproduction is an immanent character of capitalistic production, since the production of goods never corresponds to the logic of human beings' concrete needs, but to the abstract logic of the production of value. Yet in the domain of Semiocapitalism the specific overproduction that occurs is a semiotic one: an infinite excess of signs circulating in the Infosphere. Individual and collective attention is saturated.

With time, Baudrillard's intuition proved its relevance. The dominant pathology of the future will not be produced by repression, but instead by the injunction to express, which will become a generalized obligation.

When we deal with the present malaise affecting the first connective generation, we are not in the conceptual domain described by Freud in his *Civilization and Its Discontents*. Freud's vision places repression at the origin of pathology: something is hidden from us, suppressed and repressed. Something is forbidden.

Today it seems evident that seclusion is no longer at the origin of pathology, but rather hyper-vision, the excess of visibility accompanying the explosion of Infosphere: the excess of info-nervous stimulation.

Not repression, but hyper-expressivity is the technological and anthropological context framing our understanding of today's psychopathologies: ADD, dyslexia, panic. These pathologies refer to a different way of elaborating the informational input, yet they manifest themselves through pain, discomfort and marginalization.

I'd like to state here—even if this may seem superfluous—that my discourse has nothing to do with the reactionary and bigoted preaching about the bad results of permissive attitudes, and how positive the repression of the good old days was both for the intellect and for social mores.

We have seen then, how the dominant social psychopathology, identified as neurosis and described as a consequence of repression by Freud, today needs to be described as a psychosis associated with the dimension of action and an excess of energy and information.

In his schizoanalytic work, Guattari focused on the possibility of redefining the relation between neurosis and psychosis, beginning with the methodological and cognitive role of schizophrenia. This new definition had an extremely powerful political effect, coinciding with the explosion of the neurotic limits that capitalism had imposed on expression by forcing activity within the repressive limits of labor and subjugating desire to disciplinary forms of repression. But the very schizomorphic pressure of the social movements and the expressive explosion of the social led to a metamorphosis (a schizometamorphosis) of social languages, productive forms, and finally of capitalist exploitation.

The psychopathologies now spreading in the daily life of the first generations of the connective era cannot be understood at all from the standpoint of the repressive and disciplinary paradigm. These are not pathologies of repression, but of the *just do it*.

From a semio-pathological point of view, schizophrenia can be considered an excess of semiotic flows with respect to the brain's ability to interpret them. Once the universe starts running too fast, and too many signs ask to be interpreted, our mind can no longer distinguish the lines and dots giving shape to things. This is when we try to give a possible meaning through an over-inclusive process, through an extension of the limits of meaning. We will quote again, here, the conclusion of their last book written in common, *What is Philosophy?*, by Deleuze and Guattari:

> "We require just a little order to protect us from chaos. Nothing is more distressing than a thought that escapes itself, than ideas that fly off, that disappear hardly formed, already eroded by forgetfulness. They are infinite speeds that blend into the immobility of the colorless and silent nothingness they traverse, without nature or thought."[38]

## The semiotics of schizophrenia

A semiotic regime can be defined as repressive because one and only one meaning can be attributed to each and every signifier inside it. Woe to those who don't interpret properly the signs of power, who don't salute the flag, who don't respect hierarchy and the law. The semiotic regime in which we all live, we inhabitants of the semiocapitalistic universe, is characterized by the excessive velocity of signifiers and therefore it stimulates a sort of interpretative hyper-kinesis.

*Over-inclusion*, the main characteristic of schizophrenic interpretation, becomes the dominant modality of navigation in the video-electronic media proliferating universe.

In his chapter *Towards an Ecology of Schizophrenia*, Bateson thus defines schizophrenic interpretation:

> "The schizophrenic exhibits weakness in three areas of such function: (*a*) He has difficulty in assigning the correct communicational mode to the messages he receives from other persons. (*b*) He has difficulty in assigning the correct communicational mode to those messages which he himself utters or emits non-verbally. (*c*) He has difficulty in assigning the correct communicational mode to his own thoughts, sensations and percepts."[39]

In the video-electronic infosphere we all exist under the conditions that describe schizophrenic communication. The human receiver, overtaxed with signifying impulses and incapable of elaborating sequentially the meaning of enunciations and stimuli, is affected precisely by the three difficulties that Bateson is talking about. He also mentions another schizophrenic attitude, that of not being able to distinguish between metaphor and literal expression.

"The peculiarity of the schizophrenic is not that he uses metaphors, but that he uses *unlabeled* metaphors."[40]

In the universe of digital simulation the metaphor and the thing are less and less distinct: the thing becomes metaphor and the metaphor thing. Representation replaces life, and life representation. Semiotic flows and the circulation of goods overlap their codes, becoming a part of that same constellation defined by Baudrillard as "hyperreal." Therefore the schizophrenic register becomes the prevalent interpretative code. The collective cognitive system loses its critical competence, which consisted in being able to distinguish the true or false value of enunciations sequentially presented to its more or less conscious attention. In the proliferating universe of fast media, interpretation occurs according to spirals of associations and connections without signification, and no longer according to sequential lines.

In an essay entitled "Learner-Based Listening and Technological Authenticity," Richard Robin, a researcher at the George Washington University, studies the effects produced in listening comprehension by an acceleration in vocal emission. Robin founds his research in the calculation of how many syllables per second are uttered by the transmitter. The more accelerated the emission, the more syllables are pronounced, the least successful is the listening comprehension. The faster the emission, the less time is left for the listener's critical elaboration of the message. Emission's velocity and the quantity of semiotic impulses sent in a time unit are a function of the time available to the receiver for elaborating consciously.

According to Robin:

"Fast delivery rates intimidate listeners [...]. There is evidence that globalization has resulted in increased delivery tempos in areas of the world where Western broadcasting styles have replaced traditional authoritative styles. In the former Soviet Union, for example, delivery as measured in syllables per second has nearly doubled since the fall of communism from three to about six syllables per second (Robin, 1991). Casual comparisons for news broadcasts in places such as the Middle East and China lead to similar conclusions."[41]

Robin's remarks have stunningly interesting implications, helping us understand the passage from a form of authoritarian power of a "persuasive" kind (as was the case of twentieth century totalitarian regimes) to a form of biopolitical power of a "pervasive" kind (as in contemporary Info-cracy). The first is based on consent: citizens need to understand well the reasons of their President, General, Führer, Secretary or Duce. Only one source of information is authorized. Dissident voices are censured.

The infocratic regime of Semiocapital founds instead its power on overloading: accelerating semiotic flows which let sources of information proliferate until they become the white noise of the indistinguishable, of the irrelevant, of the unintelligible.

This is why we repeat that if in modern society the vastly prevalent pathology was repression-induced neurosis, today the most widely spread pathologies assume a psychotic, panic-driven character. The hyper-stimulation of attention reduces the capacity for critical sequential interpretation, but also the time available for the emotional elaboration of the other, of his or her body and voice, that tries to be understood without ever succeeding.

# 4

# The Precarious Soul

### Deregulation and control

Baudrillard remarks that the word liberation has been losing its meaning since power stopped being founded on the norm, on the disciplinary regulation of bodies and of social, linguistic and moral relations, that is to say since the world was submerged by generalized indeterminacy.

In the Fordist era, the fluctuations of prices, salaries, and profits were founded on the relation between the time of socially necessary labor and the determination of value. With the introduction of micro-electronic technologies, and the consequent intellectualization of productive labor, the relationships between existing units of measure and the different productive forces entered a regime of indeterminacy. The *deregulation* launched by Margaret Thatcher and Ronald Reagan at the beginning of the 1980s is not the cause of such indeterminacy, but its political inscription. Neoliberalism registered the end of the rule of value, and made it into an economic policy. The decision that Richard Nixon made in 1971 to delink the dollar from gold gave American capitalism a pivotal role within the global economy, freeing it from the constitutional frame established in Bretton Woods in 1944. Since then, the American economy was no longer subject to the control of economic laws (if this control ever existed), and only relied on force.

American debt could grow indefinitely, since the debtor was militarily stronger than the creditor. Since then, the USA has made the rest of the world pay for the ramping up of their war machine, and uses its war machine to threaten the rest of the world and force it to pay. Far from being an objective science, economics revealed itself to be a modeling of social relations, an enterprise of violent coercion, whose task is the imposition of arbitrary rules on social activities: competition, maximum profit, unlimited growth.

In *Symbolic Exchange and Death*, Baudrillard had an intuition about the general lines of the evolution characterizing the end of the millennium:

> "The reality principle corresponded to a certain stage of the law of value. Today the whole system is swamped by indeterminacy, and every reality is absorbed by the hyperreality of the code and simulation."[1]

The entire system fell into indeterminacy, since the correspondences between referent and sign, simulation and event, value and time of labor were no longer guaranteed. The decision that inaugurated the end of the dollar's convertibility inaugurated an aleatory regime of fluctuating values. The rule of convertibility was dismissed according to an act of political will, while in those same 1970s, the entire technical and organizational system ruled by the mechanical paradigm, started to crumble.

How is value established, then, within the aleatory regime of fluctuating values? Through violence, swindling and lies. Brute force is legitimated as the only effective source of law. The aleatory regime of fluctuating values coincides with the domination of cynicism in public discourse and in the public soul.

In order to understand the social effects of Neoliberal deregulation we have to understand the psychopathogenic effects that the precariousness of social relations produces on the individual and the collective soul. Beginning with the 1970s, *deregulation* assumed a central role in the ideology of power, upsetting not only the relations between the economy and society, but also the coordinates of critical discourse. The word *deregulation* is false. It looks as if it originated in the history of anti-systemic avant-gardes to bring a libertarian wind into the social sphere and heralding the end of every norm and constrictive rule. In reality, the deregulatory practices that accompany the victory of monetary neo-liberalism consist in clearing away all rules, so that only the rules of the economic dominate, uncontested. The only legitimate rule is now the strictest, the most violent, the most cynical, the most irrational of all the rules: the law of economic jungle.

In the works that Foucault devoted to the genealogy of modern power formations, the key concept was discipline, understood as the modeling of the bodies in the Fordist context. In his early writings, where he studied the formation of the modern disciplinary structures—mental hospitals, clinics, prisons—Foucault built a theory of modern power that included a theory of subject formation.

Now that the despotic regime of liberalist deregulation has fully developed itself, the discourse Foucault developed in his early writings needs to be updated. Foucault himself realized it, as we can see in *The Birth of Biopolitics*, the subsequently published form of his 1979 seminar at the *College de France*. Here Foucault retraces the post-Fordist transformation as an implosive insertion of the neo-liberalist form within the animated social body. In his seminar, contemporary with the election of Margaret Thatcher in Great Britain and of Ronald Reagan in the USA, Foucault broadens the scope of his genealogical and biopolitical perspective in order to include the economic processes that in those years were only beginning to take shape.

In his *Course Summary*, Foucault writes:

> "The theme was to have been 'biopolitics,' by which I meant the attempt, starting from the eighteenth century, to rationalize the problems posed to governmental practice by phenomena characteristic of a set of living beings forming a population: health, hygiene, birthrate, life expectancy, race…We know the increasing importance of these problems since the nineteenth century, and the political and economic issues they have raised up to the present."[2]

With the word biopolitics, Foucault introduces the idea that the history of power is the story of the living body being modeled by deeply mutational institutions and practices, capable of introducing behaviors and expectations and indeed permanent modifications in the living. Biopolitics represents a morphogenetic modeling of the living operated by the habitat with which it is required to interact.

Liberalism (or rather neo-liberalism, since we want to refer to the particularly aggressive variant of liberalism that was proposed throughout the 1970s by the Chicago School of economics and later adopted by American and British governments until it finally became, after 1989, the central dogma of global politics) is a political program whose purpose implies the inoculation of the enterprise principle to every space of human relations. Privatization and the fact that every fragment of the social sphere was reduced to the entrepreneurial model freed economic dynamics from any tie, be they political, social, ethical, juridical, unionist or environmental. In prior decades, these ties were able to shore up privatization, thanks to the public investment policies that had been stimulated by Keynes' reforms and the workers' organized action.

But the more liberal deregulation eliminates any legal ties within production and the juridical person is freed from regulations, the more living social time is caught in linguistic, technological and psychological chains. Foucault explains that biopolitics is a process of internalization: economic chains are incorporated in the physical and linguistic sphere once society has been freed from any formal rule. In this sense the question of freedom today is a biopolitical problem.

Let me indulge, now, in a Marxist digression.

In his so-called "Unpublished Sixth Chapter" of Volume I of *Capital*, published in the 1960s, Marx talks about the passage from formal to real subsumption by capital. Formal subsumption is based on the juridical subjugation of the laborers, on the formal disciplining of the bodies. Real subsumption means instead that the workers' lifetimes have been captured by the capital flow, and the souls have been pervaded by techno-linguistic chains.

The introduction of pervasive technologies, the computerization of productive processes and of social communication enact a molecular domination upon the collective nervous network. This is the domain of the dead object, the commodity, which objectifies human activity reducing it to a cognitive automatism. In this sense we should speak of "thanato-politics" (from the Greek "*thanatos*," meaning death): the submission of intelligent life to the dead object, the domination of the dead over the living.

Neo-Liberal theories reduce the concept of freedom to its formal, juridical dimension. But contemporary totalitarianism has forged chains that are different from those of political absolutism: its instruments of domination have moved from the domain of politics to that of the technical production of subjectivity, from the realm of the juridical person to the animated body, to the soul.

Neoliberalism aimed, on one side, at the elimination of all legal norms and social regulations that resulted in the limitation of competitive dynamics. On the other side, it wanted to transform every domain of social life (included health care, education, sexuality, affects, culture, etc) into an economic space where the only valid rule is that of supply and demand within an increasingly absolute privatization of services.

Neoliberalism eliminated the ties that protected society from the economical dynamics of competition; therefore an effect of biopolitical branding was produced in the collective mind-body.

> "It means generalizing the 'enterprise' from within the social body or social fabric; it means taking this social fabric and arranging things so that it can be broken down, subdivided, and reduced, not according to the grain of individuals, but according to the grain of enterprises. The individual life must be lodged [...] within the framework of a multiplicity of diverse enterprises connected up to and entangled with each other [...]. And finally, the individual's life itself—with his relationships to his private property, for example, with his family, household, insurance, and retirement—must make him into a sort of permanent and multiple enterprise [...]. What is the function of this generalization of the 'enterprise' form? On the one hand, of course, it involves extending the

> economic model of supply and demand and investment-costs-profit so as to make it a model of social relations and of existence itself, a form of relationship of the individual to himself, time, those around him, the group, and the family [...]. The return to the enterprise is therefore at once an economic policy or a policy of the economization of the entire social field, but at the same time a policy which presents itself or seeks to be a kind of *Vitalpolitik* with the function of compensating for what is cold, impassive, calculating, rational, and mechanical in the strictly economic game of competition."³

The reign of the enterprise is at once a political deregulation process and an epistemic process of a new segmentation of time, and cultural expectations. In this sense it is a *Vitalpolitik*, a politics of life, a biopolitics.

On a political level, the neoliberal victory leads to the creation of what Foucault defines:

> "a sort of economic tribunal that claims to assess government action in strictly economic and market terms."⁴

Every government choice, social initiative, form of culture, education, innovation, is judged according to a unique criterion: that of economic competition and profitability. Every discipline, knowledge, nuance of sensibility must conform to that criterion. Neoliberalism represents an attempt to build the *homo oeconomicus*: an anthropological model incapable of distinguishing between one's own good and economic interest.

At the origins of the liberalist vision there is a reduction of human good (ethical and aesthetic good) to economic interest, and the reduction of the idea of wealth to that of ownership. The idea of wealth is separated from the pleasure of free enjoyment and reduced to the accumulation of value.

## Becoming precarious

Within the aleatory regime of fluctuant values, precariousness becomes the general form of social existence. Capital can buy fractals of human time, recombining them through the digital network. Digitalized info-labor can be recombined in a different location, far from the one that produces it. From the standpoint of capital's valorization, the flow is continuous, finding its unity in the produced object. Yet from the cognitive workers' perspective the work done has a fragmentary character: it consists in fractions of cellular time available for productive recombination. Intermittent work cells turn on and off within the large control frame of global production. The distribution of time can thus be separated from the physical and juridical person of the worker. Social labor time is like an ocean of value producing cells that can be grouped and recombined according to capital's needs. Precariousness has changed the social composition, and the psychological, relational, linguistic, expressive forms of the new generations now facing the job market.

Precariousness is not a particular element of the social relation, but the dark core of the capitalist production in the sphere of the global network where a flow of fragmented recombinant info-labor continuously circulates. Precariousness is the transformative element of the whole cycle of production. Nobody is shielded from it. The wages of workers on permanent contracts are lowered and broken down; everyone's life is threatened by an increasing instability.

Ever since Fordist discipline was dissolved, individuals find themselves in a condition of apparent freedom. Nobody forces them to endure subjection and dependency. Coercion is instead embedded in the technicalities of social relations, and control is exerted through the voluntary yet inevitable submission to a chain of automatisms. In the U.S.A., the great majority of students need to obtain a loan in order to pay their courses and obtain a university degree. The cost of tuition is so high that this loan becomes a burden from which students can't free themselves for decades. In this way, the conditions for a new form of dependence are produced in the lives of the new generations.

The neoliberal values presented in the 1980s and 1990s as vectors of independence and self-entrepreneurship, revealed themselves to be manifestations of a new form of slavery producing social insecurity and most of all a psychological catastrophe. The soul, once wandering and unpredictable, must now follow functional paths in order to become compatible with the system of operative exchanges structuring the productive ensemble. The soul hardens, and loses its tenderness and malleability. Industrial factories used the body, forcing it to leave the soul outside of the assembly line, so that the worker looked like a soulless body. The immaterial factory asks instead to place our very souls at its disposal: intelligence, sensibility, creativity and language. The useless body lies flabbily at the borders of the game field: to take care of it and entertain it, we put it through the commercial circuits of fitness and sex.

When we move into the sphere of info-labor, Capital no longer recruits people, it buys packets of time, separated from their interchangeable and contingent bearers. De-personalized time is now the real agent of the process of valorization, and de-personalized time has no rights.

Meanwhile, the human machine is there, pulsating and available, like a brain-sprawl in waiting. The extension of time is meticulously cellular: cells of productive time can be mobilized in punctual, casual and fragmentary forms. The recombination of these fragments is automatically realized in the digital networks. The mobile phone makes possible the connection between the needs of semio-capital and the mobilization of the living labor of cyber-space. The ringtone of the mobile phone calls the workers to reconnect their abstract time to the reticular flows.

Thanks to the interconnection of its living parts, the social system seems to get more and more similar to a biological system. In 1993, in his book *Out of Control*, Kevin Kelly talked about vivisystems, artificial systems functioning according to the bio-recombining paradigm of living organisms. The general horizon traced by this book is the Global Mind, where we find synthesized biological organisms and digital networks. The global mind is a bio-digital super-organism connecting brains, bodies and electronic networks. The model of the network is able to organize and direct productive energies in the most functional way. Therefore the model of horizontal integration tends to replace that of hierarchical decision, and the model of recombination tends to replace that of the accumulation of events and dialectic contradiction. Living systems are infinitely more complex than any system that could be interpreted according to the sequential model of mechanics and of rational and voluntary action. Technology led us to produce artificial living systems. This makes the method and episteme of modern politics, which was derived from a mechanical metaphor, irreparably obsolete. We need to rethink politics according to the metaphorical possibilities of a bioinformatics model.

This idea was largely popular in cyber-culture during the 1990s: the horizontal connection of networked systems gives human intelligence a superior power. But what is the principle that semiotizes this power? And who really benefits from the empowering of the collective intelligence? In *Out of Control*, Kevin Kelly writes:

> "As very large webs penetrate the made world, we see the first glimpses of what emerges from the net-machines that become alive, smart, and evolve—a neo-biological civilization. There is a sense in which a global mind also emerges in a network culture. The global mind is the union of computer and nature—of telephones and human brains and more. It is a very large complexity of indeterminate shape governed by an invisible hand of its own."[5]

In Kelly's vision the obscure yet superior designs of the global mind are manifested through automatic mechanisms of global interactive decision making. The multitude can speak hundreds of thousands of languages, but the language that enables it to function as an integrated whole is that of the economic automatisms embodied in technology. Seized in a game of mirrors of indeterminacy and precariousness, the multitude manifests its dark side and follows automatisms that turn its wealth into misery, its power into anguish and its creativity into dependency.

The multitude does not manifest itself as autonomy at all, but rather as dependence from the automatisms that biopower builds and activates in everyday life, in our sensibility and psyche: we become a swarm. According to Eugene Thacker, a swarm is an organization of multiple, individuated units with some relation to one another.⁶ That is, a swarm is a particular kind of collectivity or group phenomenon that may be dependent upon a condition of connectivity. A swarm is a collectivity that is defined by relationality. This pertains as much to the level of the individual unit as it does to the overall organization of the swarm. At some level "living networks" and "swarms" overlap. A swarm is a whole that is more than the sum of its parts, but it is also a heterogeneous whole. In the swarm, the parts are not subservient to the whole—both exist simultaneously and because of each other.

The swarm has no political soul, only an automatic and relational soul.

The effective exercise of politics (that is to say of political government) presupposes a conscious possibility of elaborating of the information collectively shared by the social organism. But the information circulating within digital society is too much: too fast, too intense, too thick and complex for individuals or groups to elaborate it consciously, critically, reasonably, with the necessary time to make a decision. Therefore the decision is left to automatisms, and the social organism seems to function ever more often according to evolutionary rules of an automatic kind, inscribed in the genetic cognitive patrimony of individuals. The swarm now tends to become the dominant form of human action. Displacement and direction are more and more decided by the system of collective automatisms that impose themselves over the individual.

In *Business @ The Speed of Thought*, referring to the general biologic form that the process of digital production is assuming, Bill Gates writes:

> "An organization's nervous system has parallels with our human nervous system. Every business, regardless of industry,

> has 'autonomic' systems, the operational processes that just have to go on if the company is to survive [...]. What has been missing are links between information that resemble the interconnected neurons in the brain [...] You know you have built an excellent digital nervous system when information flows through your organization as quickly and naturally as thought in a human being and when you can use technology to marshal and coordinate teams of people as quickly as you can focus an individual on an issue. It's business at the speed of thought."[7]

In the connected world, the retroactive loops of a general systems theory is combined with the dynamic logic of biogenetics in a post-human vision of digital production. The model of bio-info-production imagined by Gates is the interface that will allow human bodies to integrate with the digital circuit. Once it gets fully operative, the digital nervous system can be rapidly installed on a new form of organization. Microsoft deals with products and services only apparently. In reality, it deals with a form of cybernetic organization that—once installed—structures the flows of digital information through the nervous systems of all key institutions of contemporary life. Microsoft needs to be considered a virtual memory that we can download, ready to be installed in the bio-informatics interfaces of the social organism: a cyber-Panopticon installed inside the bodily circuits of human subjectivity, a mutagenic factor introduced in the circuits of social communication. Cybernetics finally becomes life or—as Gates likes to say—information is our "vital lymph."

Biotechnologies open the way to an ulterior evolution of this scenario, allowing us to connect individual bodies and the social body with mutagenic fluxes produced by bioengineering: medications, artificial organs, genetic mutations and functional reprogramming. In a sense, even information technologies occupy the mind with mutagenic flows, invading our attention, imagination and memory. Informatics and biotechnical technologies allow bodies to connect in a continuum ruled by automatisms..

In the disciplinary society whose epistemic and practical origins were discussed by Michel Foucault, bodies were disciplined in a repressive way by social and productive rules that required consensus, submission and conscious interiorization. The law imposed by the modern state over individuals had an exterior character with respect to the conscious human organism, represented by the citizen.

The society of control, as discussed by Deleuze, is instead installed beginning with the wiring of bodies and minds, innerving automatisms of a techno-linguistic kind, thanks to mutations induced according to the finalities inscribed in the technological device. Refined technologies are active on a molecular level, they are nano-factors of mutation. Therefore they create the conditions for the control of the agent-subject through techno-linguistic automatisms and techno-operations. The minds of conscious individual organisms are connected by mutagenic flows of a semiotic kind: they transform organisms into terminals for the global mind and the bio-digital super organism.

Darwin thought that the process of selection worked on the extremely long times necessary to the natural evolution of the species. In the span of one generation we cannot perceive anything significant in this sense, and selection is manifested only in a cumulative way, throughout many generations. Little, almost imperceptible modifications are cumulated throughout extremely long temporal cycles. But is this still the case in the modern epoch?

Isn't technology a factor of incredible acceleration in the mutational processes that in nature were so slow, and hasn't it now acquired the tendency to accelerate up to the point of fully manifesting its results within one or two generations? Isn't the mutation occurring under our eyes spreading from the technological level (digitalization, connectivity) to the social, cultural aesthetic, cognitive and physiological one? Can't we see already in action the mutation of the emotional system, desiring regimes, territorial dislocations, modalities of attention, memorization and imagination? Aren't we beginning to perceive a possible psychological mutation in the organism, induced by biotechnology?

Therefore it is true that the environment has a determinant function on the choices made by human minds, yet human minds are part of the environment. For this reason, the conclusions that liberalist theory elaborated from the premises of social Darwinism follow a pseudo-logic. It is true that biology dominates human action, but human action also determines biology. The question is to understand which choices (epistemic, technologic and finally instinctual and aesthetic) a conscious human mind will make.

**The modeling of the soul**

Modern society was founded on the perspective of a human government over a world built on a human scale. This government must discipline bodies, communicational relations and language. Discipline as Foucault suggested already in his *History of Madness*, implies the reduction of the world to reason, while at the same time irrationality is confined, segregated, repressed and medicalized. The development of the Fordist industrial form presupposes the same disciplining process, while also redefining it. The productive relation between body and machine was formed through a slow interaction which was visible, conscious and governable. The anatomical body and the capitalistic macro-machine are reciprocally modeled throughout this process. In the Fordist factory, anatomy and mechanics keep together the system of productive bodies which occupy the material space of objects, transformations and displacements. In this material and visible space, labor and conflict become manifest, and power is organized.

But once the digital appears on the horizon of social life, the central factors of social relations move from the analogical domain (of sizes, bodies, drives) to that of algorithms (relations, constants, simulations). Digitalization implies a shift at the essential level of manipulation: social products are no longer manipulated materially, but they are generated at a conceptual level. The site where productive, social and communicative series are established is isolated from social knowledge and even visibility. On the social scene automatisms are expressed, yet the domain where they are produced is subtracted from visibility, not only because this is a clandestine domain (laboratories of research are subtracted from any democratic judgment or decision), but also because everything happens within nanotechnology.

The humanistic horizon was related to Protagoras' premise that "man is the measure of all things." In the traditional—even in the industrial—world, man is the measure, and the technologic universe is built upon his will and concrete capacities to manipulate. This is no longer true once the technologies of the invisible spread. The important "things" (indeed they are generative algorithms) that count and determine the formation of social phenomena no longer correspond to a human measure: the human eye can no longer perceive them. Politics is weakened, since all that is given in the politically visible has no value, it is pure "spectacle": while spectacle is what we can see, generative algorithms are invisible. Domination therefore shifts from the domain of bodily, mechanical and political disciplining to that of logical and psychological, or logical and biogenic automatisms. Not the body but the soul becomes the subject of techno-social domination. Capitalist globalization is supported essentially by these techno-linguistic automatisms, diffused and connected at a general level in productive society, so that capitalist valorization becomes more and more independent from any conscious activity and the very possibility of human political action.

The political extinction of the working class was not and is not a consequence of any struggle between political forces, or the effect of a social elimination. Workers continue to exist, but their social action is no longer effective in relation to the dominant processes that are actually producing general social effects. What has irreversibly changed on the scene of Semiocapital is the relationship between the human factor (the workers) and sites of control and decision. Control is no longer exerted on a macrosocial or anatomic level, as bodily constriction. Control is exerted at an invisible, irreversible level, a level that cannot be ruled, since it happens through the creation of linguistic and operative automatisms structuring the way the technosphere functions.

Control over the body is no longer exerted by molar mechanisms of constriction, but by micro machines that are incorporated into the organism through psychopharmacology, mass communication and the predisposition of informatics interfaces. That means that control over the body is exerted by the modeling of the soul.

## Bioinformatics ontology

Pico della Mirandola was a humanist and philologist who, in 1486, wrote a text entitled *Oratio de dignitate hominis*. Here I am quoting from his work:

> "Now the highest Father, God the master-builder, had, by the laws of his secret wisdom, fabricated this house, this world which we see, a very superb temple of divinity. He had adorned the super-celestial region with minds. He had animated the celestial globes with eternal souls; he had filled with a diverse throng of animals the cast-off and residual parts of the lower world. But, with the work finished, the Artisan desired that there be someone to reckon up the reason of such a big work, to love its beauty, and to wonder at its greatness. Accordingly, now that all things had been completed [...], He lastly considered creating man. But there was nothing in the archetypes from which He could mold a new sprout, nor anything in His storehouse which He could bestow as a heritage upon a new son, nor was there an empty judiciary seat where this contemplator of the universe could sit. Everything was filled up; all things had been laid out in the highest, the lowest, and the middle orders. But it did not belong to the paternal power to have failed in the final parturition [...]; it did not belong to wisdom, in a case of necessity, to have been tossed back and forth through want of a plan; it did not belong to the loving-kindness which was going to praise divine liberality in others to be forced to condemn itself. Finally, the best of workmen decided that that to which nothing of its very own could be given should be, in composite fashion, whatsoever

had belonged individually to each and every thing. Therefore He took up man, a work of indeterminate form; and, placing him at the midpoint of the world, He spoke to him as follows:

'We have given to thee, Adam, no fixed seat, no form of thy very own, no gift peculiarly thine, that thou mayest feel as thine own, have as thine own, possess as thine own the seat, the form, the gifts which thou thyself shalt desire. A limited nature in other creatures is confined within the laws written down by Us. In conformity with thy free judgment, in whose hands I have placed thee, thou art confined by no bounds; and thou wilt fix limits of nature for thyself. I have placed thee at the center of the world, that from there thou mayest more conveniently look around and see whatsoever is in the world. Neither heavenly nor earthly, neither mortal nor immortal have We made thee. Thou, like a judge appointed for being honorable, art the molder and maker of thyself; thou mayest sculpt thyself into whatever shape thou dost prefer. Thou canst grow downward into the lower natures which are brutes. Thou canst again grow upward from thy soul's reason into the higher natures which are divine.'"[8]

Writing his speech on human dignity at the end of the fifteenth century, Pico inaugurated the modern horizon: the exercise of human power is not established by any archetype, norm or necessity, since the Creator did not determine in any way the path that s/he needs to follow. In those same years a newly Christianized Spain expelled Muslims and Jews from its territories, and armies of Christian Spaniards brought to the new continent a civilization of death, extermination and abuse. Access to modernity was marked by an assertion of freedom and enterprise that was also an imposition of violence.

Pico tells us that God had no more archetypes available and that the human creature, the favorite one, the last and most complex, could not be defined by any archetype or essence. God had therefore to leave humans their freedom to define themselves, freely establishing the limits of their acts and destiny. Human becoming was not delimited or finalized by divine will, but was left to the will of human indeterminacy. Freedom is understood as freedom from determinacy: in this sense, it is constitutive of human essence.

Modernity was inaugurated by this awareness: human civilization is a project, not the development or the realization of a design, implicit in divine will or in Being. The history of modernity played itself out in the emptiness of Being. But in the historical manifestations of this constant overcoming of limits, modernity reaches both its apex and exhaustion.

The technical development of human intelligence creates the conditions for putting under critical light the very indeterminacy that Pico stressed as the essential and original character of the human being. Despite the fact that human freedom had been guaranteed by the divine decision to let humans live with their own indeterminacy, free to define themselves, Technology suspends and obliterates human freedom, building a destiny that is objectified and embodied in the linguistic automatism.

In his *Letter on Humanism*,[9] Heidegger already shows how humanism is in danger: it is actually condemned by the "beyond the human" that is implicit in the mathematization and digitalization of knowledge, and by the automatization of life. The will to power produced the instruments of its own end, and the end of human freedom, that is to say the quintessentially human: since the human is situated in a space of freedom that technology eliminates.

> "More essential than instituting rules is that man find the way to his abode in the truth of Being [...]. Thus language is at once the house of Being and the home of human beings. Only because language is the home of the essence of man can historical mankind and human beings not be at home in their language, so that for them language becomes a mere container for their sundry preoccupations."[10]

Language is the house of Being, but at the same time Heidegger tells us that language belongs to technique: technique becomes at once its privileged object and the subject that produces, enunciates, programs.

> "The fundamental event of modernity is the conquest of the world as picture. From now on the word 'picture' means: the collective image of representing production [...]. For the sake of this battle of world views, and accordingly to its meaning, humanity sets in motion, with respect to everything, the unlimited process of calculation, planning, and breeding. Science as research is the indispensable form taken by this self-establishment in the world; it is one of the pathways along which, with a speed unrecognized by those who are involved, modernity races towards the fulfillment of its essence."[11]

The last words in this quote need some attention. After having said that modernity is the conquest and submission of the world as a picture finally reduced to an integrated form, Heidegger comes to the conclusion that this process takes place at a speed unrecognized by those who are involved.

But who are they? They are human beings, little by little deprived of the authority to rule the world, and replaced by the automatisms which penetrate the world and redefine it. Heidegger says that human beings ("those involved") cannot recognize the speed with which modernity races towards the fulfillment of its essence, since this fulfillment is precisely the unawareness of human beings, their dependency on automatisms. Humans are less and less aware of the process that they themselves initiated. Thanks to their freedom, born from the distance between Being and existent, and the ontologically unprejudiced character of existence, humanity came to the point of realizing a technical realm installed in the empty place of Being. The empty place of Being is thus filled by the performative power of the technosphere, and the numeric convention is transformed into an operational device.

The end of Humanism stems from the power of Humanism itself.

# Conclusion

**The genesis of the present depression**

The collapse of the global economy can be read as the return of the soul. The perfect machine of Neoliberal ideology, based on the rational balance of economic factors, is falling to bits because it was based on the flawed assumption that the soul can be reduced to mere rationality. The dark side of the soul—fear, anxiety, panic and depression—has finally surfaced after looming for a decade in the shadow of the much touted victory and the promised eternity of capitalism.

In this short conclusion I want to consider two different meanings of the word depression.

By this word we mean a special kind of mental suffering, but also the general shape of the global crisis that is darkening the historical horizon of our time. This is not simple wordplay, this is not only a metaphor, but the interweaving and interacting of psychological flows and economic processes.

In the year 2000 the American market experienced the effects of an overproduction in the Info-economical field. After the dotcom crash, and the breakdown of big corporations like WorldCom, Enron and so on, American capitalism changed the course of its development, and the economy of virtual production gave way to the war economy. Thanks to the war, the economy restarted, but the cost of labor continued to fall and the growth was in fact based on the expansion of private and public debt. The overproduction crisis did not go away, and finally showed up again in 2008, after the subprime crisis triggered the most astounding of financial crashes.

The events of economic depression and of psychic depression have to be understood in the same context: they are interrelated not only because they are feeding off each other, but also because psychoanalytic theory has something to teach social thinkers, and psychotherapy may suggest very useful methods for processes of social transformation.

Neoliberal ideology is based on the idea that an economy can be conceived as a balanced system of rational expectations and of rational investments. But in the social space not all expectations are rational, and not all investments are "economic" in a mathematical, scientific sense. Desire is involved in the process, and the Unconscious is speaking behind the curtains of every investment scene, of any act of consumption and economic exchange.

This is why the supposedly perfect balance of the market has become a catastrophic mess.

Euphoria, competition, and exuberance were all involved in the dynamics of the bull market years. Panic and depression were denied, but they were always at work. Now they are re-surfacing and disturbing the normal flow of capitalist valorization.

Semiocapitalism, the production and exchange of semiotic matters, has always exploited the soul as both productive force and market place. But the soul is much more unpredictable than the muscular workforce which was at work in the assembly line.

In the years of the Prozac economy the soul was happy to be exploited. But this could not last forever. "Soul troubles" first appeared in the last year of the dotcom decade, when a techno-apocalypse was announced under the name of Millennium bug. The social imagination was so full of apocalyptic expectations that the myth of a global techno-crash created a thrilling wave all around the world. Nothing happened on Millennium night, but the global psyche teetered for a moment on the brink of the abyss.

In those days, Alan Greenspan was talking of irrational exuberance, in order to pinpoint the dangerous effects of emotional disturbances in the field of the financial markets. But these disturbances were not an accident, a contingent temporary phenomenon: they were the effect of the hyper-exploitation of our psychological energy; they were collateral damage, the unavoidable consequence of the soul at work. In reality, it is impossible to avoid the spreading of emotionality, it is impossible to avoid the effects of psychopathologies when the nervous energies of the cognitarian work force are submitted to unremitting info-stimulation.

The fear of a depression materialized in the spring of 2000, when the virtual economy suddenly was jeopardized by the plunge taken by the high-tech stock market. The dotcom bubble burst and the overall economy was so deeply shocked that rumors of depression started to spread all around the world.

But how do you treat a depression?

Would you try to heal it with amphetamines, with a shock-therapy of stimulating psychotropic medicines? Only a foolish doctor would do this, but unfortunately such a character really happened to sit in the Oval Office of the White House, and an amphetamine therapy was prescribed by George W. Bush in the form of war and tax reductions for the wealthy. Bush issued an invitation to go shopping, and actually facilitated an unprecedented increase in private and public debt.

At the same time, a campaign was launched worldwide against collective intelligence, against freedom of research, against public schools.

In the long run, a depression treatment based on artificially-induced euphoria will not work, and sooner or later the depressed organism will collapse. The emphasis on competitive lifestyles and the permanent excitation of the nervous system prepared the final collapse of the global economy which is now unfolding under the eyes of an astonished mankind.

The Neoliberal ideal of an inherent balance among the various components of the economic system was a flawed theory because it did not consider the systemic effects of the social mind. Therefore, the bipolar economy swung from euphoria to panic, and is now teetering on the brink of a deep depression.

**Beyond our knowledge**

Economists and politicians are worried: they call it a crisis, and they hope that it will evolve like the many previous crises that disrupted the economy in the past century but finally went away, leaving Capitalism stronger.

I think that this time is different. This is not a crisis, but the final collapse of a system that has lasted five hundred years.

Look at the current landscape: the big world powers are trying to rescue the financial institutions, but the financial collapse has already affected the industrial system: demand is falling, jobs have been lost by the millions. In order to rescue the banks, the State is forced to take money from tomorrow's taxpayers, and this means that in the coming years demand is going to fall further. Family spending is plummeting, and consequently much of the current industrial production will have to cease.

In an article recently published by the *International Herald Tribune*, the moderate-conservative David Brooks wrote:

> "I worry that we are operating far beyond our economic knowledge."

This is precisely the point: the complexity of the global economy is far beyond any knowledge and possible governance.

Presenting the Obama rescue plan on February 10, 2009, the American Secretary of the Treasury, Timothy Geithner, said:

> "I want to be candid. This comprehensive strategy will cost money, involve risk and take time. We will have to adapt it as conditions change. We will have to try things we've never tried before. We will make mistakes. We will go through periods in which things get worse and progress is uneven or interrupted."

Although these words show the intellectual honesty of Geithner, and the impressive difference of the new leading American class compared to the Bushites, they do point toward a real breakdown in political self-confidence.

The political and economic knowledge we have inherited from modern rationalist philosophy is now useless, because the current collapse is the effect of the infinite complexity of immaterial production and of the incompatibility or unfitness of the general intellect when confronted with the framework of capitalist governance and private property.

Chaos (i.e. a degree of complexity which is beyond the ability of human understanding) now rules the world. Chaos means a reality which is too complex to be reduced to our current paradigms of understanding. The capitalist paradigm can no longer be the universal rule of human activity.

We should not look at the current recession only from an economic point of view. We must see it as an anthropological turning point that is going to change the distribution of world resources and of world power. The model based on growth has been deeply interiorized, since it pervaded daily life, perception, needs, and consumption styles. But growth is over and will never be back, not only because people will never be able to pay for the debt accumulated during the past three decades, but also because the physical planetary resources are close to exhaustion and the social brain is on the verge of collapse.

**Catastrophe and morphogenesis**

The process underway cannot be defined as a crisis. Crisis means the destructuration and restructuration of an organism which is nonetheless able to keep its functional structure. I don't think that we will see any re-adjustment of the capitalist global structure. We have entered a major process of catastrophic morphogenesis. The capitalist paradigm, based on the connection between revenue and work performance is unable to frame (semiotically and socially) the present configuration of the general intellect.

In the 1930s the opportunity for a New Deal rested on the availability of physical resources and in the possibility of increasing individual demand and consumption. All that is over. The planet is running out of natural resources and the world is heading towards an environmental catastrophe. The present economic downturn and the fall in oil prices are feeding the depletion and exhaustion of planetary resources.

At the same time we cannot predict any boom in individual consumption, at least in the Western societies. So it is simply nonsensical to expect an end to this crisis, or a new policy of full employment. There will be no full employment in the future.

The crash in the global economy is not only an effect of the bursting of the financial bubble. It is also and primarily an effect of the bursting of the work bubble. We have been working too much during the last five centuries, this is the simple truth. Working so much has implied an abandonment of vital social functions and a commodification of language, affections, teaching, therapy and self-care.

Society does not need more work, more jobs, more competition. On the contrary: we need a massive reduction in work-time, a prodigious liberation of life from the social factory, in order to reweave the fabric of the social relation. Ending the connection between work and revenue will enable a huge release of energy for social tasks that can no longer be conceived as a part of the economy and should once again become forms of life.

As demand shrinks and factories close, people suffer from a lack of money and cannot buy what is needed for everyday life. This is a vicious circle that the economists know very well but are completely unable to break, because it is the double bind that the economy is doomed to feed. The double bind of over-production cannot be solved by economic means, but only by an anthropological shift, by the abandonment of the economic framework of income in exchange for work. We have simultaneously an excess of value and a shrinking of demand. A redistribution of wealth is urgently needed. The idea that income should be the reward for a performance is a dogma we must absolutely get rid of. Every person has the right to receive the amount of money that is needed for survival. And work has nothing to do with this.

Wages are not a natural given, but the product of a specific cultural modeling of the social sphere: linking survival and subordination to the process of exploitation was a necessity of capitalist growth. Now we need to allow people to release their knowledge, intelligence, affects. This is today's wealth, not compulsive useless labor. Until the majority of mankind is free from the connection between income and work, misery and war will be the norm of the social relationship.

**How to heal a depression?**

Although they seldom, if ever, used the "D" word, Félix Guattari and Gilles Deleuze say very interesting things on the subject in their last books, *Chaosmosis*, and *What is Philosophy?* In the final chapter of *What is Philosophy?* they speak of Chaos. Chaos, in their words, has very much to do with the acceleration of the semiosphere and the thickening of the info-crust. The acceleration of the surrounding world of signs, symbols and info-stimulation is producing panic, as I have already said in the previous parts of this book. Depression is the deactivation of desire after a panicked acceleration. When you are no longer able to understand the flow of information stimulating your brain, you tend to desert the field of communication, disabling any intellectual and psychological response. Let's go back to a quote that we have already used:

> "Nothing is more distressing than a thought that escapes itself, than ideas that fly off, that disappear hardly formed, already

eroded by forgetfulness or precipitated into others that we no longer master."[1]

We should not see depression as a mere pathology, but also as a form of knowledge. James Hillman says that depression is a condition in which the mind faces the knowledge of impermanence and death. Suffering, imperfection, senility, decomposition: this is the truth that you can see from a depressive point of view.

In the introduction to *What is Philosophy?* Deleuze and Guattari speak of friendship. They suggest that friendship is the way to overcome depression, because friendship means sharing a sense, sharing a view and a common rhythm: a common refrain (*ritournelle*) in Guattari's parlance.

In *Chaosmosis* Guattari speaks of the "heterogenetic comprehension of subjectivity":

> "Daniel Stern, in *The Interpersonal World of the Infant*, has notably explored the pre-verbal subjective formations of infants. He shows that there are not at all a matter of 'stages' in the Freudian sense, but of levels of subjectivation which maintain themselves in parallel through life. He thus rejects the overrated psychogenesis of Freudian complexes, which have been presented as the structural 'Universals' of subjectivity. Furthermore he emphasizes the inherently trans-subjective character of an infant's early experiences."[2]

The singularity of psychogenesis is central in Guattari's schizoanalytic vision. This implies also the singularity of the therapeutic process.

> "It's not simply a matter of remodeling a patient's subjectivity—as it existed before a psychotic crisis—but of a production sui generis... these complexes actually offer people diverse possibilities for recomposing their existential corporeality, to get out of their repetitive impasses and, in a certain way to resingularize themselves."[3]

These few lines must be read, in my opinion, not only as a psychotherapeutic manifesto but also as a political one.

The goal of schizoanalysis is not, in Guattari's words, to reinstall the universal norm in the patient's behavior, but to singularize him/her, to help him/her becoming conscious of his or her difference, to give him/her the ability to be in good stead with his being different and his actual possibilities.

When dealing with a depression the problem is not to bring the depressed person back to normality, to reintegrate behavior in the universal standards of normal social language. The goal is to change the focus of his/her depressive attention, to re-focalize, to deterritorialize the mind and the expressive flow. Depression is based on the hardening of one's existential refrain, on its obsessive repetition. The depressed person is unable to go out, to leave the repetitive refrain and s/he keeps going back into the labyrinth.

The goal of the schizoanalyst is to give him/her the possibility of seeing other landscapes, to change focus, to open new paths of imagination.

I see a similarity between this schizoanalytic wisdom and the Kuhnian concept of paradigmatic shift which needs to occur when scientific knowledge is taken inside a conundrum. In *The Structure of Scientific Revolutions* (1962) Kuhn defines a paradigm as "a constellation of beliefs shared by a group of people." A paradigm may therefore be seen as a model which gives way to the understanding of a certain set of realities. A scientific revolution in Kuhn's vision is the creation of a new model which fits the changing reality better than the previous epistemic models.

The word "episteme" in the Greek language means to stand in front of something: the epistemic paradigm is a model that allows us to face reality. A paradigm is a bridge which gives friends the ability to traverse the abyss of non-being.

Overcoming depression implies some simple steps: the deterritorialization of the obsessive refrain, the re-focalization and change of the landscape of desire, but also the creation of a new constellation of shared beliefs, the common perception of a new psychological environment and the construction of a new model of relationship.

Deleuze and Guattari say that philosophy is the discipline that involves creating concepts. In the same way, they argue that schizoanalysis is the discipline that involves creating percepts and affects through the deterritorialization of obsessive frameworks.

In the current situation, the schizoanalytic method should be applied as political therapy: the Bipolar Economy is falling into a deep depression. What happened during the first decade of the century can be described in psychopathological terms, in terms of panic and depression. Panic happens when things start swirling around too quickly, when we can no longer grasp their meaning, their economic value in the competitive world of capitalist exchange. Panic happens when the speed and complexity of the surrounding flow of information exceed the ability of the social brain to decode and predict. In this case desire withdraws its investments, and this withdrawal gives way to depression.

Here we are, after the subprime crack and the following global collapse.

Now what?

The economic collapse cannot be solved with the tools of economic thought, because economic conceptualization is in fact the problem and not the solution.

The strict correlation between income and labor, the fanatical pursuit of growth, the dogmas of compatibility and competition: these are the pathogenic features that our social culture must get rid of, if we want to come out of our depression. In the dominant political discourse, the overcoming of a depression means restarting the dynamics of growth and consumption: this is what they call "recovery." But this will be impossible both because the collective debt cannot be paid and because the planet cannot support a new phase of capitalist expansion. The economy of growth is itself the poison. It cannot be the antidote.

Over the last ten years, the French anthropologist Serge Latouche has been talking of *décroissance* (Degrowth) as a political goal. But now *décroissance* is simply a fact: when the Gross National Product is falling everywhere, entire sections of the industrial system are crumbling and demand is plummeting, we can say that degrowth is no longer a program for the future. Degrowth is here.

The problem is that social culture is not ready for this, because our social organization is based on the idea of the interminable expansion of consumption, and the modern soul has been shaped by the concept of privatization and by the affects of an unending increase in consumption.

The very notion of wealth has to be reconsidered: not only the concept of wealth, but the perception of being rich. The identification of wealth with purchasing power is deeply embedded in the social psyche and affectivity. But a different understanding of wealth is possible, one that is not based on possession, but on enjoyment. I'm not thinking of an ascetic turn in the collective perception of wealth. I think that sensual pleasure will always be the foundation of well-being. But what is pleasure? The disciplinary culture of modernity has equated pleasure and possessing. Economic thinking has created scarcity and has privatized social need, in order to make possible the process of capitalist accumulation. Therein lies the source of the current depression.

**The interminable process of therapy**

We should not expect a swift change in the social landscape, but rather the slow surfacing of new trends: communities will abandon the field of the crumbling economy; more and more individuals will abandon their job searches and will start creating extra-economic networks of survival.

The very perception of well being and of being rich will change in the direction of frugality and freedom.

The de-privatization of services and goods will be made possible by this much-needed cultural revolution. This will not happen in a planned and uniform manner. It will be the effect of the withdrawal of singular individuals and communities and of the creation of an economy based on the sharing of common things and services and on the liberation of time for culture, pleasure and affection.

The identification of well-being with private property is so deeply rooted that we cannot absolutely rule out the eventuality of a barbarization of the human environment. But the task of the general intellect is precisely this: to escape from paranoia, to create zones of human resistance, to experiment with autonomous forms of production based on high-tech/low-energy models, to interpellate the people with a language that is more therapeutic than political.

In the days to come, politics and therapy will be one and the same. The people will feel hopeless and depressed and panicked, because they can't deal with the post-growth economy and they will miss our dissolving modern identity. Our cultural task will be to attend to these people and to take care of their trauma showing them the way to pursue the happy adaptation at hand. Our task will be the creation of social zones of human resistance, zones of therapeutic contagion. Capitalism will not disappear from the global landscape, but it will lose its pervasive, paradigmatic role in our semiotization, it will become one of possible form of social organization. Communism will never be the principle of a new totalization, but one of the possible forms of autonomy from capitalist rule.

In the 1960s, Castoriadis and his friends published a magazine whose title was: *Socialism or Barbarism*.

But you will recall that in *Rhizome*, the introduction to *A Thousand Plateaus*, Deleuze and Guattari argue that the disjunction (or...or...or) is precisely the dominant mode of Western Metaphysics that we are trying to forget. They oppose this disjunctive model with a conjunctive approach:

> "A rhizome has no beginning or end, but it is always a middle, between things, interbeing, *intermezzo*. The tree is filiation, but the rhizome is alliance, uniquely alliance. The tree imposes the verb 'to be,' but the fabric of the rhizome is the conjunction, 'and ... and ... and ...' This conjunction carries enough force to shake and uproot the verb 'to be' [...] to establish a

logic of the AND, overthrow ontology, do away with foundations, nullify endings and beginnings."[4]

The process of autonomy should not be seen as *Aufhebung*, but as Therapy. In this sense, it is neither totalizing and nor it is intended to destroy and abolish the past.

In a letter to his master, Sigmund Freud, the young psychoanalyst Fliess asked when it is possible to consider a therapy to be over and the patient be told, "you are ok." Freud answered that the psychoanalysis has reached its goal when the person understands that therapy is an interminable process.

Autonomy is also a process without end.

# Notes

### Introduction

1. *The Philosophy of Epicurus*, translated by Gorge K. Strodach, Evanston: Northwestern University Press (1963), pp. 128–129.

### 1. Labor and Alienation in the philosophy of the 1960s

1. Karl Marx, *Theses on Feuerbach* in Karl Marx, (with Friederich Engels), *The German Ideology*, Prometheus Books: New York, (1998), p. 574.

2. Jean-Paul Sartre, "A Plea for Intellectuals," translated by John Matthews, in *Between Existentialism and Marxism*, New York: Pantheon, (1974), pp. 228–231.

3. Karl Marx, *The Grundrisse*, edited and translated by David McLellan, New York: Harper Torchbooks, (1972), p. 143.

4. http://www.marxists.org/archive/marx/works/1844/manuscripts/labour.htm.

5. *Ibid.*

6. *Ibid.*

7. *Hegel and the Human Spirit: A Translation of the Jena Lectures on the Philosophy of Spirit (1805–1806)* with commentary by Leo Rauch, Detroit: Wayne State University Press, (1983), p. 120.

8. G. W. F. Hegel, *The Phenomenology of Spirit*, translated by A.V. Miler, Oxford University Press (1977), p. 10.

9. Martin Jay, *The Dialectical Imagination: A History of the Frankfurt School and the Institute of Social Research 1923–1950*, Toronto, Little Brown & Company, (1973), p 274.

10. Herbert Marcuse, *Reason and Revolution: Hegel and the Rise of Social Theory*, London, New York: Oxford University Press, (1941), p. 277.

11. http://www.marxists.org/archive/marx/works/1844/manuscripts/labour.htm.

12. Mario Tronti, *Operai e capitale*, Torino: Einaudi (1973), p. 261; "The Struggle Against Labor," *Radical America*, Volume 6, number 3 (May-June 1972), pp. 22–23.

13. Luciano Gallino, *Nota a L'uomo a una dimensione*, Torino: Einaudi, (1967), p. 262.

14. Herbert Marcuse, *One Dimensional Man: Studies in the Ideology of Advanced Industrial Society*, Boston: Beacon Press (1966), p. 1.

15. *Ibid.*, pp. 31–32.

16. Louis Althusser [and] Etienne Balibar, *Reading "Capital,"* translated [from the French] by Ben Brewster, London: NLB, (1977), p. 17.

17. *Ibid.*, p. 34.

18. *Ibid.*, pp. 24–26.

19. *Ibid.*, p. 34.

20. Karl Marx, *The Grundrisse*, op. cit., pp. 100–101.

21. *Ibid.*, p. 104.

22. Karl Marx, *Capital: a Critique of Political Economy*, Vol. 1, translated by Ben Fowkes, London: Penguin, (1976), p. 128.

23. *Ibid.*, p. 166.

24. Karl Marx, *The Grundrisse*, op. cit. p. 693.

25. *Ibid.*, pp. 693–694.

26. *Ibid.*, p. 701.

27. *Ibid.*, pp. 705–706.

28. *Ibid.*, pp. 142–143.

29. See Gregory Bateson, "Toward a Theory of Schizophrenia," in *Steps to an Ecology of Mind: Collected Essays in Anthropology, Psychiatry, Evolution, and Epistemology*, Chicago: University Of Chicago Press (1972).

30. Hans Jürgen Krahl, *Konstitution und Klassenkampf*, Frankfurt: Neue Kritik, (1971).

31. Hans Jürgen Krahl, *Konstitution und Klassenkampf, op. cit.*, p. 357, translated by Giuseppina Mecchia, *cfr*. Franco Berardi (Bifo), "Technology and Knowledge in a Universe of Indetermination," *SubStance*, #112, Vol 36, no. 1, 2007.

32. *Ibid.*, p, 365.

33. *Ibid.*, p. 365.

34. *Ibid.*, p. 367.

35. Herbert Marcuse, *One Dimensional Man: Studies in the Ideology of Advanced Industrial Society, op. cit.*, pp. 86–87. Marcuse is quoting (*cfr*. footnotes 4 and 5) Stanley Gerr, "Language and Science," in *Philosophy of Science*, April 1942, p. 156.

36. *Ibid.*, p. 123.

37. *Ibid.*, p. 159.

38. *Ibid.*, pp. 168–169.

## 2. The Soul at Work

1. Alain Ehrenberg. *La fatigue d'être soi: dépression et société*, Paris: Editions Odile Jacob, (1998), p. 10.

2. *Ibid.*, p. 18, *English version by the translator.*

## 3. The Poisoned Soul

1. Robin, Léon, *Greek Thought and the Origins of the Scientific Spirit*, translated from the new revised and corrected French edition by M. R. Dobie, New York: Russell & Russell, (1967), p. 113.

2. Félix Guattari, *Chaosmosis, an Ethico-Aesthetic Paradigm*, translated by Paul Brains and Julian Pefanis. Bloomington: Indiana University Press, (1995), p. 83.

3. Gilles Deleuze, Félix Guattari, *What is Philosophy?* Translated by Hugh Tomlinson and Graham Burchell. New York: Columbia University Press, (1994), p. 208.

4. Unpublished in English. Selected essays from *Psychanalyse et transversalité* (1972) and *La révolution moléculaire* (1977) have been published in Félix Guattari, *Molecular Revolution: Psychiatry and Politics*, translated by Rosemary Sheed, New York: Penguin, (1984).

5. Félix Guattari, *Chaosmosis, an Ethico-Aesthetic Paradigm, op. cit*, p. 135.

6. Gilles Deleuze, Félix Guattari, *What is Philosophy?, op. cit.*, p. 201.

7. *Ibid.*, p. 201.

8. *Ibid.*, pp. 213–214.

9. *Ibid.*, p. 203.

10. *Ibid.*, pp. 204–205.

11. Félix Guattari, *Chaosmosis, an Ethico-Aesthetic Paradigm, op. cit*, pp. 112–113.

12. Gilles Deleuze, Félix Guattari, *What is Philosophy?, op. cit.*, p. 205.

13. Félix Guattari, *Chaosmosis, an Ethico-Aesthetic Paradigm, op. cit*, pp. 10–11.

14. *Ibid.*, p. 18.

15. Roland Barthes, *Empire of Signs*, translated by Richard Howard, New York: Hill and Wang, (1982), pp. 27–28.

16. Jean Baudrillard, *The Ecstasy of Communication*, translated by John Johnson, in *The Anti-Aesthetic, Essays in Post-Modern Culture*, edited by Hal Foster, Port

Townsend, Wash: Bay Press, (1983), p. 126. Baudrillard refers here to his first book: *Le Système des objects*, Paris: Gallimard, (1968).

17. Jean Baudrillard, *The Illusion of the End*, translated by Chris Turner, Cambridge: Polity Press (1994), p. 15.

18. Jean Baudrillard, *America*, London-New York: Verso (1989), p. 29.

19. Jean Baudrillard, *Forget Foucault*, in Jean Baudrillard, *Forget Foucault & Forget Baudrillard: an Interview with Sylvère Lotringer*, New York, Semiotext(e), (1987), p. 17.

20. *Ibid.*, pp. 17–19.

21. "Run comrade, the old world is behind you."

22. Jean Baudrillard, *Forget Foucault, in Jean Baudrillard, Forget Foucault & Forget Baudrillard: an interview with Sylvère Lotringer*, op. cit., p. 25.

23. Jean Baudrillard, *In the Shadow of the Silent Majorities, or, The End of the Social, and Other Essays*, translated by Paul Foss, Paul Patton and John Johnston, New York: Semiotext(e), (1983), p. 44.

24. Jean Baudrillard, *The Illusion of the End*, op. cit., p. 17.

25. Jean Baudrillard, *In the Shadow of the Silent Majorities, or, The End of the Social, and Other Essays*, op. cit., p. 46.

26. Gilles Deleuze, *Expressionism in Philosophy: Spinoza*, translated by Martin Joughin, New York: Zone Books, (1990), p. 28.

27. *Ibid.*, pp. 119–120.

28. Gilles Deleuze, Félix Guattari, *What is Philosophy?*, op. cit., p. 201.

29. Jean Baudrillard, *In the Shadow of the Silent Majorities, or, The end of the Social, and Other Essays*, op. cit., pp. 60–61.

30. Jean Baudrillard, *Symbolic Exchange and Death*, translated by Iain Hamilton Grant, with an introduction by Mike Gane, London: Sage, (1993), p. 4.

31. Jean Baudrillard, *The Illusion of the End*, op. cit., p. 1.

32. *Ibid.*, p. 19.

33. Jean Baudrillard, *Symbolic Exchange and Death, op. cit.*, p.69.

34. Jean Baudrillard, *The Spirit of Terrorism and Other Essays*, translated by Chris Turner. London, New York: Verso (2003), pp. 3–4.

35. Sigmund Freud, *Civilization and its Discontents*, translated from the German and edited by James Strachey, New York: W.W. Norton, (1962), p. 44.

36. *Ibid.*, p. 60.

37. Jean Baudrillard, *The Intelligence of Evil or the Lucidity Pact*, translated by Chris Turner, Oxford, New York: Berg, (2005), p. 27.

38. Gilles Deleuze, Félix Guattari, *What is Philosophy?, op. cit.*, p. 201.

39. Gregory Bateson, *Steps to an Ecology of Mind*, New York: Ballantine (1972), p. 205.

40. *Ibid.*

41. Richard Robin, "Learner-Based Listening and Technological Authenticity," in *Language Learning & Technology*, vol. 11, n° 1, February, (2007), pp. 109–115.

## 4. The Precarious Soul

1. Jean Baudrillard, *Symbolic Exchange and Death, op. cit.*, p. 2.

2. Michel Foucault, 1926–1984, *The Birth of Biopolitics: Lectures at the Collège de France, 1978–79*, edited by Michel Senellart, translated by Graham Burchell. Basingstoke [England], New York: Palgrave Macmillan (2008), p. 317.

3. *Ibid.*, pp. 241–242.

4. *Ibid.*, p. 247.

5. Kevin Kelly, *Out of Control: The New Biology of Machines, Social Systems and the Economic World*, Addison Wesley (1994), p. 1.

6. Eugene Thacker: "Networks, Swarms, Multitudes," CTHEORY (May 2004).

7. Bill Gates with Collins Hemingway, *Business @ the Speed of Thought: Using a Digital Nervous System*, New York, NY: Warner Books, (1999), pp. 23–38.

8. Giovanni Pico della Mirandola, *On the Dignity of Man and Other Works*, translated by Charles Glenn Wallis, with an introduction by Paul J.W. Miller, Indianapolis: Bobbs-Merrill (1965), pp. 4–5.

9. Martin Heidegger, "Letter on Humanism," in *Basic Writings: From* Being and Time *(1927) to* The Task of Thinking *(1964)*, with general introduction and introductions to each selection by David Farrell Krell, New York: Harper & Row, (1977), p. 207.

10. *Ibid.*, pp. 238–239.

11. Martin Heidegger, *Off the Beaten Track*, edited and translated by Julian Young and Kenneth Haynes, New York: Cambridge University Press (2002), p. 71.

**Conclusion**

1. Gilles Deleuze, Félix Guattari, *What is Philosophy?*, *op. cit.*, p. 201.

2. Félix Guattari, *Chaosmosis, an Ethico-Aesthetic Paradigm*, *op. cit.*, p. 6.

3. *Ibid.* pp. 6–7.

4. Gilles Deleuze, Félix Guattari, *A Thousand Plateaus.* Translated by Brian Massumi. London and New York: Continuum, (2004), p. 25.

# SEMIOTEXT(E) Post-Political Politics

### AUTONOMIA
**Post-Political Politics**
Edited by Sylvère Lotringer and Christian Marazzi

Semiotext(e) has reissued in book form its legendary magazine issue *Autonomia: Post-Political Politics*, originally published in New York in 1980. Edited by Sylvère Lotringer and Christian Marazzi with the direct participation of the main leaders and theorists of the Autonomist movement (including Antonio Negri, Mario Tronti, Franco Piperno, Oreste Scalzone, Paolo Virno, Sergio Bologna, and Franco Berardi), this volume is the only first-hand document and contemporaneous analysis that exists of the most innovative post-'68 radical movement in the West.

7 x 10 • 340 pages • ISBN: 978-1-58435-053-8 • $24.95

### CAPITAL AND LANGUAGE
**From the New Economy to the War Economy**
Christian Marazzi, translated by Gregory Conti
Introduction by Michael Hardt

*Capital and Language* takes as its starting point the fact that the extreme volatility of financial markets is generally attributed to the discrepancy between the "real economy" (that of material goods produced and sold) and the more speculative monetary-financial economy. But this distinction has long ceased to apply in the postfordist New Economy, in which both spheres are structurally affected by language and communication. Marazzi points to capitalism's fourth stage (after mercantilism, industrialism, and the postfordist culmination of the New Economy): the "War Economy" that is already upon us.

6 x 9 • 180 pages • ISBN: 978-1-58435-067-5 • $14.95

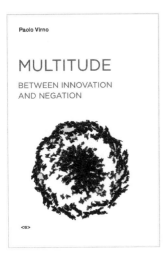

## MULTITUDE BETWEEN INNOVATION AND NEGATION
Paolo Virno, Translated by Isabella Bertoletti, James Cascaito, and Andrea Casson

*Multitude between Innovation and Negation* offers three essays that take the reader on a journey through the political philosophy of language.

"Wit and Innovative Action" explores the ambivalence inevitably arising when the semiotic and the semantic, grammar and experience, rule and regularity, and right and fact intersect. "Mirror Neurons, Linguistic Negation, and Mutual Recognition" examines the relationship of language and intersubjective empathy: without language, would human beings be able to recognize other members of their species? And finally, in "Multitude and Evil," Virno challenges the distinction between the state of nature and civil society and argues for a political institution that resembles language in its ability to be at once nature and history.

6 x 9 • 200 pages • ISBN: 978-1-58435-050-7 • $14.95

## THE PORCELAIN WORKSHOP
### For a New Grammar of Politics
Antonio Negri, Translated by Noura Wedell

In 2004 and 2005, Antonio Negri held ten workshops at the Collège International de Philosophie in Paris to formulate a new political grammar of the postmodern. Biopolitics, biopowers, control, the multitude, people, war, borders, dependency and interdependency, state, nation, the common, difference, resistance, subjective rights, revolution, freedom, democracy: these are just a few of the themes Negri addressed in these experimental laboratories.

Postmodernity, Negri suggests, can be described as a "porcelain workshop": a delicate and fragile construction that could be destroyed through one clumsy act. Looking across twentieth century history, Negri warns that our inability to anticipate future developments has already placed coming generations in serious jeopardy.

6 x 9 • 224 pages • ISBN: 978-1-58435-056-9 • $17.95